# JANE AUSTEN
## FOR BEGINNERS

# JANE AUSTEN
## FOR BEGINNERS

**BY ROBERT G. DRYDEN • ILLUSTRATIONS BY JOE LEE**

**FOR BEGINNERS®**

*an imprint of Steerforth Press*
*Hanover, New Hampshire*

For Beginners LLC
155 Main Street, Suite 211
Danbury, CT 06810 USA
www.forbeginnersbooks.com

Text ©2012 Robert G. Dryden
Illustrations ©2012 Joe Lee

A For Beginners® Documentary Comic Book
Copyright © 2012

Cataloging-in-Publication information is available from the Library of Congress.

ISBN # 978-1-934389-61-4 Trade

Manufactured in the United States of America

For Beginners® and Beginners Documentary Comic Books® are published by For Beginners LLC.

First Edition

10 9 8 7 6 5 4 3 2 1

# contents

# Preface

Greetings and welcome to *Jane Austen for Beginners*.
In these pages you will find discussions of Austen's
six major novels. Along with sustained looks at *Sense
and Sensibility, Pride and Prejudice, Mansfield Park,
Emma, Northanger Abbey*, and *Persuasion*, I also
provide an overview of Austen's life and times, speculation about her legacy, and a roundup of numerous
Austen-related films and TV productions, book
spinoffs, Austen-fan websites, and more,
generated by the tidal wave of Jane Austen enthusiasm that has swept the English-speaking
world and beyond in the past twenty-plus years.

This book is for everyone who is curious about
Jane Austen. If you have no intention of reading
the novels but want to hold your own in Austen
conversations, this book is for you. If you are
a student or general reader attempting to
tackle the novels for the first time, this book
is for you. If you read Austen a long time ago
but don't remember much, this book is for
you. And if you are a knowledgeable Austen
aficionado, please read on for perspectives
I hope you find new and interesting.

Kindly note that in my engagement with
the novels, I reveal significant portions of the
plots. If you want to let the plotlines in
Austen's books unfold organically, begin your reading with the novel introductions, then turn to the novels
themselves. These overviews will help you
with the big picture—contexts, characters, historical
background, and themes. Once you have finished reading the novels, go back and complete the chapters. What
you find in them will help illuminate central plotlines

1

and open up new vistas to enhance your understanding of and pleasure in Jane Austen's brilliant fiction.

*Jane Austen for Beginners* is intended to complement and contribute to the world of discussion concerning our friend Jane. Sophisticated content is conveyed in an accessible style that will help the beginning Austen reader understand the novels at an advanced level. But as you read, keep in mind that there is no single manual or key to understanding Jane Austen's books. There is no single Austen "authority." Reading and thinking about great literature is so rewarding because interpretations are manifold. Since no book could possibly address all interpretations of Austen's work, consider these discussions part of the dialogue.

My work here represents nearly twenty years of contemplation of Jane Austen and her fiction. I included Austen in my Ph.D. dissertation, I have published scholarly articles on aspects of Austen's life and novels, I have taught Austen's novels at the college level, and I have enjoyed reading these novels as a member of the general reading public. The amount of scholarship on Jane Austen is staggering. In keeping with the style and format of the *For Beginners* series, I have not used a formal citation style in my discussions, nor do I cite page numbers when quoting from her fiction. On occasion I do refer by title or name to sources and scholars that figure prominently into a particular discussion. I have also provided in my bibliography a list of texts that have been useful to me during my long courtship of Jane Austen. These resources along with my suggestions for further reading will be useful to the Austen reader who is not satisfied to sit still after completing this book. Enjoy!

*Robert G. Dryden*

# Chapter 1

# Introduction

Jane Austen's impact on late twentieth and early twenty-first-century American, British, and even global audiences is so immense that it's hard to fathom. Austenmania has become an industry, and Austen's popularity today is arguably eclipsed only by interest in the Bard himself, William Shakespeare. With our contemporary knowledge of what a phenomenon Jane Austen has turned out to be, we should find it surprising (to say the least) that at the time of her death, her own brothers and sister initially suppressed Jane's identity as author. When she passed away in the town of Winchester, England in 1817, and her body was carried over from 8 College Street to the spot that had been reserved for her in the mighty Winchester Cathedral, her epitaph did not mention that Jane Austen was a writer. It mentions the "extraordinary endowments of her mind" and the "sweetness of her temper," but nowhere in the brief three paragraphs is there even a reference to the fact that this woman completed six novels and that at the time of her death she had published four of them. In fact, Jane Austen died in relative obscurity, and knowledge about the precise facts of her life remains somewhat murky. With all that is written about her today—the hundreds of texts that claim to know Jane Austen so intimately—you would think that her life had been the subject of a reality show. But that was hardly the case.

For starters we're not sure what Jane Austen looked like. There was no family portrait commissioned, and aside from one sketch of Austen that was drawn by the amateur hand of her sister Cassandra (a second sketch by Cassandra doesn't show Jane's face), Jane was never the subject of an artist's rendition. There is one recollection by her nephew James Edward Austen-Leigh, who writes fifty years after Austen's passing in his *A Memoir of Jane Austen and Other Family Recollections*:

> In person she was very attractive; her figure was rather tall and slender, her step light and firm, and her whole appearance expressive of health and animation. In complexion she was a clear brunette with a rich colour; she had full round cheeks, with mouth and nose small and well formed, bright hazel eyes, and brown hair forming natural curls close round her face.

Austen-Leigh's somewhat generic description of Jane Austen is lovely, but it's all we have. It is also imparted to us by a nephew who hadn't seen his aunt in fifty years! Taking into consideration the great span of elapsed time, we have to accept that Austen's precise likeness will forever remain a mystery.

Adding to the ambiguity about her personal history is the horrifying fact that Austen's sister Cassandra (who outlived Jane by twenty-eight years) burned an estimated 2800 letters from Jane before passing away in 1845. Can you imagine how much was lost? Countless insights into Jane Austen the person—her likes and dislikes, daily activities, daydreams, fantasies, fears, troubles—are all gone forever.

. . .

And then there is the suspect biographical information we have about Austen written by those who knew her. Late in 1817, the year of Austen's death, her brother Henry Austen penned a "Biographical Notice" as a forward to Jane's posthumously published works, *Northanger Abbey* and *Persuasion*. In this biography, Henry begins to reinvent his sister and deify her in a likeness that people refer to as "Saint Jane." As an example, her brother states that his sister was "Faultless . . . as nearly as human nature can be" and that she "sought, in the faults of others,

5

something to excuse, to forgive or forget." Henry paints his sister as religiously devout and incapable of behaving in any way that could be deemed negative. The love Henry shows for his sister is touching, but we can't help seriously question the veracity of this biographical portrait. And if Jane Austen was so faultless, why would Cassandra feel compelled to burn so many of her sister's letters?

Austen's deification continued in 1870 with Austen-Leigh's memoir and family recollections. Penned so long after Jane's death, there is speculation about how much of Austen-Leigh's loving biography is rooted securely in fact. Fifty years provides a great deal of opportunity for fiction to infiltrate the facts. This is not to say that Austen's nephew intentionally sugar-coated his aunt's memory, but rather that a portrait of someone created a half century later is subject to the vagaries of recollection.

My point, as I begin to provide you with some of the biographical details of Jane Austen's life, is that there are still questions about aspects of the historical record. But that's not necessarily a bad thing. One of the reasons for Austen's immense popularity is that all the facts of her life are not etched in stone. There is so much room for speculation, and we Janeites (the term used for Austen groupies) like it that way.

• • •

# Austen Family Background

Jane Austen was born on December 16, 1775 in a town called Steventon in Hampshire, England (sixty miles south of London) to Mr. George and Mrs. Cassandra-Leigh Austen. Jane's father, who was orphaned by the time he was seven years old, was left no inheritance of property or money. Up until his early teens, he was cared for by an aunt on his father's side. At age sixteen, George Austen received a fellowship that enabled him to attend St. John's College in Oxford, and since he proved to be an excellent scholar, he stayed on to take another degree in divinity. Mr. Austen also had two successful relatives who were instrumental in helping him establish a career as a country parson: Mr. Francis Austen and Mr. Thomas Knight. By the time George Austen completed his schooling at Oxford, he received gifts of two rectories: one in the village of Steventon given to him by Mr. Knight, and the other in Deane given to him by his uncle Mr. Austen. After marrying Cassandra Leigh at St. Swithin's Church in Bath in 1764, the couple immediately set out for Hampshire. They initially lived at the parsonage in Deane, but after four years moved over to the rectory at Steventon. They would never be rich, but they enjoyed a respectable social rank at the lower level of the gentry. In his memoir, J. E. Austen-Leigh recalls that George Austen was a handsome and charismatic man, and Jane's mother had an acute intellect and excelled at both writing and conversation. George Austen took up the occupations of pastor and teacher for the two small communities in Hampshire and the couple commenced production of a large family. George Austen received a modest living from his work and stuck with it until he retired at the age of 70. The church at Steventon where George Austen preached and where the Austen family worshiped still stands to this day, but the rectory where they lived was torn down shortly after Jane's death. All that remains on the property of the former Austen home is a metal water-pump handle that replaced the wooden one used by the Austen family.

As for brothers and sisters, Jane Austen had many—six brothers and one sister. Her eldest sibling was James, a man of letters who was ten years older than Jane. He and Mr. Austen provided young Jane with a strong educational background uncommon for a woman of her day. Like his father, James Austen was bound for a career in the clergy. He served as a curate in Hampshire for much of his career, and eventually moved his family into the Steventon rectory and took over as parson when his father retired in 1801.

The next eldest brother was George. He was omitted from most contemporary Austen family trees because he was developmentally disabled. He never learned to speak and was kept apart from the family for the majority of his life. It is believed that he may have been "deaf and dumb." Mrs. Austen had a brother who was also mentally disabled, and these two men resided together as boarders with caretakers in a nearby Hampshire town.

After George, there was Edward, who was adopted at an early age in 1783 by Mr. and Mrs. Thomas Knight of Godmersham, Kent. Practically unthinkable today, the Austens relinquished parental control of one of their children in an exchange that was beneficial for both families. The Knights had all the land, money, and prestige that could ever be wanted by an elite family of the English gentry; however, they were lacking a male heir. Through the process of adopting Edward, the Knights' line of succession was extended, and the Austens undoubtedly benefited from their now much closer connection to the Knight family. Later in his life, Edward Knight would inherit two large country estates: Godmersham Park and Chawton House in Hampshire. After the death of her father, Jane Austen would make her final residence at Chawton Cottage on the property of Edward's estate.

Jane was closest with the fourth Austen brother, Henry. He spent the first part of his career as a banker, and after losing his business, he turned in his middle age to the profession of the clergy. He had many influential business connections in high English society and was able to assist Jane in locating publishers for her novels. He aided his sister in publishing four of them during her lifetime—*Sense and Sensibility* (1811), *Pride and Prejudice* (1813), *Mansfield Park* (1814) and *Emma* (1815)—and then in the months after Jane Austen's death, Henry penned the biography of his sister and added it to the publication of a two-novel volume that included *Northanger Abbey* (completed by 1799) and *Persuasion* (December 1817, but dated 1818).

Next in terms of male siblings were Austen's two sailor brothers. The first was Francis, who served in the Royal British Navy, and during his long career he climbed to the position of Senior Admiral of the Fleet. After Frank came the last Austen son, Charles, who also had a career in the Royal Navy, although not as distinguished as Frank's. These brothers were at sea for most of their lives, but Jane maintained close contact with them through their written correspondence. Both Austen brothers were significant players in Admiral Nelson's fleet and served in the Royal Navy during heroic Napoleonic War battles. Austen invents detailed naval characters in two of her novels, *Mansfield Park* and *Persuasion*. Her depictions of these characters are highly accurate. Austen knew her way around the details of life in the Royal Navy, more so than most women of her day could be expected. Austen's detailed knowledge undoubtedly was accumulated through the intimate family connections she had with her sailor brothers. As Austen-Leigh notes, "with ships and sailors [Jane] felt herself at home, or at least could always trust to a brotherly critic to keep her right."

## Sister Cassandra and Jane Austen's Letters

Cassandra Austen was Jane's closest friend in life. She was three years older than Jane, but the two women were joined at the hip from childhood until Jane's death.

For most of their lives they resided in the same homes and shared the same bedrooms. Austen-Leigh recalls that "Cassandra's was the colder and calmer disposition; she was always prudent and well judging, but with less outward demonstration of feeling and less sunniness of temper than Jane possessed." Cassandra and Jane confided in each other throughout their lives, and when they were not together physically, they tirelessly corresponded. Even at the end of Austen's life, it was Cassandra who nursed her sister until her final seconds had expired.

At some point in the years following Jane's death, Cassandra began editing and then destroying the lion's share of Jane's letters that were in her possession. There is considerable evidence that Cassandra burned most of the correspondence that the two shared. Jane Austen wrote an estimated three thousand letters, and most were addressed to Cassandra. The belief is that Cassandra feared the prying eyes of future scholars and enthusiasts. In her censoring mission, she cut sections out of several letters, but the great majority (presumably containing what Cassandra perceived as a combination of embarrassing, private, and compromising information) she outright destroyed. Alarmingly, only 160 letters survive! Virginia Woolf explains with sadness:

It is probable that if Miss Cassandra Austen had had her way we should have had nothing of Jane Austen's except her novels. To her elder sister alone did she write freely; to her alone she confided her hopes and, if rumour is true, the one great disappointment of her life; but when Miss Cassandra Austen grew old, and the growth of her sister's fame made her suspect that a time might come when strangers would pry and scholars speculate, she burnt, at great cost to herself, every letter that could gratify their curiosity, and spared only what she judged too trivial to be of interest.

11

Cassandra's action went a long way towards eternally preventing scholars and biographers from being able to separate fact from fiction. As Woolf says, Cassandra was fearful that scholars would "speculate," and so we continue to do so. The loss of over 2800 letters leaves speculation as our primary option.

## Town and Country

Jane Austen spent most of her life in extremely rural and provincial surroundings. As her novels demonstrate, rural English communities consisted of a handful of families living within a mile or two of one another. These communities were populated by all the characters we meet in Austen's novels—the country parson, members of the country gentry, and the occasional commissioned army officer stationed nearby, or the naval midshipman, lieutenant, or captain on leave from his duty at sea. Both Steventon and Chawton (where Austen lived and wrote for the final eight years of her life) fit that description well. By most accounts, Austen preferred living a rural existence; however, there is some debate in the Austen community about her sentiments towards urban life. The prevailing opinion had for some time been that she disliked the city. We know for a fact that she did not put pen to paper when in Bath or London. But that doesn't necessarily mean that she was unhappy. Most of her novels contain important scenes set in Bath or London, so the fact that she wasn't materially productive in the city should not compel us to conclude that she was consistently unhappy.

# The Austens and the English Social Hierarchy

During the early nineteenth century, the English social hierarchy was structured as follows: Next to the king's court, the aristocracy was at the top, and it was comprised of a few hundred families of lords, dukes, viscounts, and earls, most of whom were part of the government. They derived their staggering wealth from both rents and their positions in power. They lived in sprawling country estates and huge city mansions. Since Jane Austen had no contact with members from this elite social class, aristocrats do not appear in the pages of her novels.

Below the aristocracy was the gentry, and here is where we see the majority of characters who inhabit Austen's novels. From the Elliots and Musgroves of *Persuasion* to the Bertrams of *Mansfield Park* and Tilneys of *Northanger Abbey*, these families are all in possession of estates that have been in their families for many generations. The ranking of the gentry is a bit complicated, but for the Austen beginner, suffice it to say that there are three social levels: the landed gentry, the lesser landed gentry, and the professional minor gentry. As Maggie Lane illustrates in her essay "Daily Life in Jane Austen's England," members of the landed gentry were titled in the ranks of either baronet or knight, and of those two, only the baronet's title was passed down from father to son. *Mansfield Park*'s Sir Thomas Bertram and *Persuasion*'s Sir Walter Elliot are the two representatives in Austen's novels from this class. Since the title of knight was bestowed during a person's lifetime, it could not be passed down. Both Sir William Lucas from *Pride and Prejudice* and Sir Henry Russell from *Persuasion* are knights. Correspondingly, the wives of both baronets and knights are referred to by the title Lady.

The lesser landed gentry was composed of many of the misters in Austen's stories. Examples here include Mr. Darcy of *Pride and Prejudice*, Mr. Knightly (who is a magistrate) from *Emma*, and Mr. Palmer (who is running for Parliament) from *Sense and Sensibility*. These are the higher-ranking members, but the lesser landed gentry also includes most of the families that have named estates, such as Longbourn in *Pride and Prejudice*, Hartfield in *Emma*, and Uppercross in *Persuasion*. The rank of characters in these mid-level gentry positions varies, but most of the patriarchs share in common that they are first sons living in their ancestral homes.

Finally, the professional minor gentry consisted predominantly of offspring of the landed gentry (second and third sons), who did not stand to inherit property. These individuals derived their incomes from the three professions: the church, the armed services, and the law. Countless examples of this class exist in Austen's world, and they include Austen's own father, who was a clergyman, Admiral Croft from *Persuasion*, and the Vicar Elton from *Emma*.

Jane Austen's family has been described as existing in the ranks of the "pseudo gentry" (a term coined by scholar David Spring). Since George Austen held a position in the church and had family connections with members of the landed gentry, he and his family can technically be included in the professional minor gentry, but keep in mind that these borders between social stations are in many cases somewhat fuzzy. The main reason for this lack of clarity is that the middle class, the social station beneath the Austens, is competing with the gentry for prestige in society.

The middle class—or the "new middle class" as it was called—consisted of successful, educated men who lacked breeding and connections to elite families. It comprised professionals like lawyers and doctors, officers in the army and navy (who were not from landed families), and merchants and businessmen. Due to the ambiguous boundaries between the lower level of the gentry and the upper level of the middle class, opinions differ about the extent of middle-class characters in the pages of Austen's novels. Some critics argue that members of the middle class barely exist; others (including myself) view the cast of middle-class characters as substantial, however. As we will discuss at length in most of the chapters that follow, England is evolving into the globally powerful Great Britain, and the early nineteenth century brings with it war with France, the emergence of the Industrial Revolution, and colonization. As England evolves into the British Empire, there are all kinds of personal money-making ventures to pursue, and many members of the middle class are striking while the iron is hot. As Austen demonstrates so well in all of her novels, members of this emerging middle class are competing for status in society with members of the landed gentry. One of the best examples is from *Persuasion*, where wealthy naval officers are mingling with members of the gentry. Admiral Croft rents a familial estate that the baronet, Sir Walter Elliot, can no longer afford, and a middle-class naval captain (Frederick Wentworth) eventually climbs up the social ladder by marrying the daughter (Anne Elliot) of that same baronet. We also see in *Pride and Prejudice* another excellent example of blurring of boundaries between middle class and the gentry. Charles Bingley is a member of the middle class nouveau riche. He is not landed, and the source of his fortune is never revealed, but the fact that he is extremely well-monied enables him to mingle with the likes of Fitzwilliam Darcy. More likely than not, his fortune was made in the colonial realm, where opportunities were vast. For our purposes, however, suffice it to say that in the early nineteenth century, money is competing with social rank, and like it or not, members of the gentry are opening up their doors to newly affluent members of the middle class.

## Childhood and Education

When Jane Austen was born, her parents obeyed
a custom (albeit a dying one) whereby infants were
not kept at home, but with a wet nurse. Thus,
for the better part of her first two years of life,
Austen was kept in a cottage in the village where
she was nursed and cared for. Her parents would
visit on a daily basis, and they would often bring her
home for short periods of time, but her primary care was elsewhere
until she could walk and begin to talk. Reasons for the practice varied.
Lawrence Stone in *The Family, Sex and Marriage in England 1500-1800*
states that on the one hand, mothers were freed of the drudgery of breast
feeding and the demands it placed on their bodies, but another more com-
pelling reason stemmed from husbands who wanted to maintain sexual access to their wives and did not want to compete with a nursing child.

As for education, it is not surprising that Jane Austen's was far superior to that of her peers. With older brothers, a highly intelligent mother, and a father who was a teacher, it is also not surprising that Austen's
education began very early. Austen-Leigh tells us, "In childhood every
available opportunity of instruction was made use of. According to the
ideas of the time, she was well educated, though not highly accomplished,
and she certainly enjoyed that important element of mental training, as-
sociating at home with persons of cultivated intellect." Since males exclusively received a formal education and went on to study classical Greek
and Latin, there were limits to Austen's progress as a scholar; however,
by the time she was a teenager, she was well versed in the practice of writing. She wrote stories, a few poems, and some plays. Many of these are
available, collected in a volume referred to as Jane Austen's *Juvenilia*. They
include *Love and Friendship*, *Catherine*, and *The History of England from
the Reign of Henry the 4$^{th}$ to the Death
of Charles the 1$^{st}$*. Her family home

at Steventon was the location where Austen eventually blossomed as an author. In her early twenties, Austen wrote her most successful novel, *Pride and Prejudice* (which she began and finished in a period of about ten months during the years 1796 and 1797), and she also wrote drafts of *Sense and Sensibility* and *Northanger Abbey*.

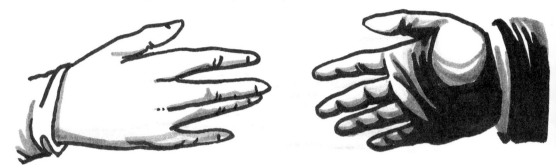

## *Romance for Cassandra and Jane*

Much has been made in the last decade about possible romances that the Austen sisters might have had during their lifetimes. Considering the tiny size of the communities where the Austens lived, the world of romance was limited at best. Since romantic options consisted of members of a few families that lived in neighboring houses within a small community, it shouldn't come as a surprise that neither Cassandra nor Jane married during their lifetimes. But for both women, there were a few close calls.

When the family still lived in Steventon, Cassandra received and accepted a proposal of marriage from a clergyman in the area, Tom Fowle, who had been a student of Mr. Austen's and had grown up with their family since childhood. Like some unfortunate characters in Austen's books, this young man was endowed with neither land nor money, but he did have a patron, a Lord Craven, who would have assisted the young Fowle in establishing himself to be a suitable groom for the marriage. Tragedy struck, however, when he followed Lord Craven to the West Indies (serving his master as a chaplain of the regiment), contracted yellow fever, and died. The news devastated Cassandra. And this was, as far as is commonly known, her sole opportunity for marriage.

Jane had never been engaged in her life, but she did have a few opportunities for marriage that never came to fruition. It is widely known in the

Janite community that, like Elizabeth Bennet in *Pride and Prejudice* (who rejects a marriage proposal from the character Mr. Collins), Jane herself rejected a marriage proposal from a prospective suitor whom she didn't care for. Austen-Leigh reports: "In her youth [Jane] had declined the address of a gentleman who had the recommendations of good character, and connections, and position in life, of everything, in fact, except the subtle power of touching her heart." The Austen reader easily comes to understand Jane's decision when we take into consideration that true love should be the ultimate criterion for marrying. However, in Austen's time most women did not have the luxury of marrying for love. You might say a woman's duty was to get married, and there were serious social consequences if she did not. In *Pride and Prejudice*, for example, Charlotte Lucas jumps at the chance to marry Mr. Collins after he had been rejected by Elizabeth Bennet. Charlotte is not in love with Collins, but (like women of the time) she is practical. It's fair to say that the majority of women in early nineteenth-century England were conditioned to think like Charlotte Lucas, not like Elizabeth Bennet or Jane Austen.

Austen-Leigh also recalls another story of prospective romance for Jane that evolved briefly when the family had been vacationing at a seaside location (possibly Devon). As he puts it, the Austens "became acquainted with a gentleman, whose charm of person, mind and manners was such that Cassandra thought him worthy to possess and likely to win her sister's love. When they parted, he expressed his intention of soon seeing them again; and Cassandra felt no doubt as to his motives. But they never again met. Within a short time they heard of his sudden death. I believe that, if Jane ever loved, it was this unnamed gentleman."

18

In addition to these accounts of near-romance in Austen's short life, there is another possible romantic encounter that is depicted in the 2007 film *Becoming Jane*, where the author falls in love with a man named Tom Lefroy. According to the Jane Austen Society of North America, there is some merit to the story depicted in the film. Apparently Austen and Lefroy met when they were each twenty during a visit Lefroy made to Hampshire to visit his aunt and uncle. Lefroy, an Irishman, was on break from studying law in London. Austen wrote a letter to her sister about her experience with Mr. Lefroy and their interaction during the course of three balls. On January 14, 1796, she writes, "I look forward with great impatience to [the ball], as I rather expect to receive an offer from my friend in the course of the evening." The engagement never came to fruition, however, and there is evidence that Mr. Lefroy became engaged two years later to a woman in Ireland, and they married the following year. They did name one of their daughters Jane (as the film depicts), but Jane was also the name of Mr. Lefroy's mother, so make of that what you will.

# Bath, England

The town of Bath was England's premier vacation and social destination during much of the eighteenth and early nineteenth centuries. Bath was a social hot spot, where fashionable people came to see and be seen. It is known for its fifteenth-century cathedral, Roman baths, natural hot springs, and beautiful Georgian architecture. Bath's culture was urban and sophisticated. There were ballrooms, a modern theater, shops, restaurants, and access to professional services every bit as good as what you could find in London. Many elders and retirees were advised to "take" the healing waters of Bath for a wide variety of illnesses. Along with this aging population, younger, unmarried men and women came to Bath to find a partner.

In 1797 Jane visited Bath for the first time, staying with an aunt and uncle. She also came for a visit in 1799. During her second visit, Austen came with her mother to see her brother Edward Knight and his family. As a vacation destination, she didn't see much wrong with Bath, and it inspired her to create the characters Catherine Morland and Henry Tilney from *Northanger Abbey*, who meet at a ball in Bath and eventually go on to marry and live happily ever after. Austen thought differently, however, when it came to the prospect of living in Bath. In the year 1800 she received word from her father that at the age of seventy he was ready to

retire, leave Steventon for good, and move the family to Bath. Having married in Bath, Jane Austen's parents viewed the town as a place of romance and fond memories. After forty years of service as a country parson in Steventon, Mr. and Mrs. Austen were ready for a change. Unfortunately Jane and Cassandra didn't share their enthusiasm; they were astounded and depressed by the announcement and had no desire to live there. As evidence of Austen's unhappy attitude about moving to Bath, biographer Claire Tomalin notes that Austen wrote four letters during her first weeks in Bath, and the tone and content suggest "a mind struggling against low spirits." The family's time in Bath came to a conclusion in 1805 with the death of Austen's father.

Following George Austen's death, Mrs. Austen, Cassandra and Jane left Bath for Southampton, where they resided for three years, living first with Francis Austen and his new wife and then in a house in Castle Square. Speculation has it that this Southampton period prolonged Jane's unhappiness. Essentially the three women were at the mercy of the Austen brothers for money and lodging. Several of the brothers pitched in to help their dependent female family members. This situation provides a good example of the kinds of difficulties unmarried women faced during this time in history. Widows and unmarried women were a charge to their families for care and necessities. At this time in their lives, Mrs. Austen and Cassandra had a total of £200 combined, and Jane, who had not yet begun to make money from her writing, had

nothing to contribute. It's also worth noting that during the seven or so years between leaving Steventon and arriving at Chawton Cottage, Austen produced little writing. Undoubtedly Austen was inventing characters and plots in her imagination, but she was not putting pen to paper. Her lack of literary output might suggest that Austen was consistently depressed, but the beginning Austen reader should keep in mind that this hypothesis is based mostly on speculation.

## *Chawton Cottage*

In 1809, following the three years in Southampton, Austen's brother Edward (the son who had been adopted into the Knight family) had the opportunity to offer his mother and sisters two different living options: one was a house on his property in Kent at Godmersham Park, the other a cottage in Chawton, just down the lane from Edward's occasional residence, Chawton House. Due to its location in Hampshire and close proximity to Steventon, the women chose Chawton Cottage and never looked back.

In terms of literary creation, these years at Chawton Cottage were the most productive for Austen, and they rivaled her time in Steventon for happiness. As Austen-Leigh says, "Chawton may be called the *second*, as well as the *last* home of Jane Austen; for during the temporary residences of the party at Bath and Southampton she was only a sojourner in a strange land, but here she found a real home amongst her own people." As Tomalin puts it, "The effect on Jane of this move to a permanent home in which she was able to re-establish her own rhythm of work was dramatic. It was as though she were restored to herself, to her imagination, to all her powers: a black cloud had lifted. Almost at once she began to work again. *Sense and Sensibility* was taken out and revisions began."

The red-brick cottage at Chawton was built in roughly 1700 as a farmhouse, and later served as an inn. As they had done at Steventon, Jane and Cassandra shared a bedroom, and the two sisters lived harmoniously with their mother. Life in Chawton was quiet, picking up only when family members had the opportunity to visit. Jane became intent on making progress with her writing, which was going extremely well. During the first year at Chawton, Jane was able to complete revisions on both *Sense and Sensibility* and *Pride and Prejudice*, and between the years 1811 and 1816 she began from scratch and completed *Mansfield Park*, *Emma*, and then finally *Persuasion*. This output is impressive, especially in light of the way that Austen had to work. She had no special office or specific quiet time for concentration and productive writing. Male writers of Austen's day would have had all the resources needed for composition, and their time and space would have been respected by family members and visitors. But lacking a room of her own (as Virginia Woolf would say), Austen had to piece together her sentences and paragraphs amidst distractions and interruptions. By the early nineteenth century, women were making strides to be taken seriously as authors, but they still had a long way to go. Thus, Austen, who did most of her writing in a general living area, wrote on small sheets of paper that could easily be concealed from the eyes of servants and guests to the house.

## Prince Regent

In 1815 Austen's brother Henry became extremely ill, and Jane hurried to his bedside in Hans Place in London in order to nurse him back to

23

health. Since Henry had been a successful banker, he had friends in high places. Thus, when Jane arrived she was introduced to a physician who was in the employ of the Prince Regent. When this physician learned the identity of his patient's sister, he informed Austen that the Prince was a fan of her novels and that he owned several copies. When the physician notified the Prince that Miss Austen was in London, the Prince made an invitation to Jane to come and visit Carlton House and meet with his librarian. The Prince's instructions to his librarian were to "show her the library and other apartments, and to pay her every possible attention." The Prince also requested that if Austen had a book in progress, that he would not object if she were to dedicate it to him. *Emma* was already at the press, but there was time to affix the dedication, and so it was done. The dedication reads: "To His Royal Highness The Prince Regent, This Work Is, By His Royal Highness's Permission, Most Respectfully Dedicated, By His Royal Highness's Dutiful And Obedient Humble Servant, The Author."

This was the extent of Jane Austen's brush with celebrity. She made a little money from the novels while she was alive, but for the most part she remained obscure and anonymous. As well, her writing never changed her life. She didn't join a literary circle, she didn't have tutorials with writer friends, and she didn't join a radical woman's group. As her nephew states:

Jane Austen lived in entire seclusion from the literary world: neither by correspondence, nor by personal intercourse was she known to any contemporary authors. It is probable . . .

> ... that she never was in company with any persons whose talents or whose celebrity equaled her own; so that her powers never could have been sharpened by collision with superior intellects, nor her imagination aided by their casual suggestions. Whatever she produced was a genuine home-made article. Even during the last two or three years of her life, when her works were rising in the estimation of the public, they did not enlarge the circle of her acquaintance. Few of her readers knew even her name, and none knew more of her than her name.

Indeed, Jane Austen's reputation took the better part of two centuries to mature. Taking into consideration the frenzy of popularity that has arisen during the last twenty years, you would think differently. Building slowly, her celebrity has finally exploded.

## Death

Jane Austen's fatal illness, thought at the time to be Addison's disease, started as a physical complaint in the year 1816. This coincided with extreme financial difficulties for Austen's brother Henry. Henry, who had made an excellent recovery after his nearly fatal illness the year before, was now suffering a monetary crisis; his bank was failing fast and would soon leave him penniless. And after his long banking career was in ruins, he, like his father and brother James before him, turned to the church.

During Henry's crisis, Austen was busy working on a novel that she was calling "The Elliots" (the working title for her last novel published under the name *Persuasion*). She was feeling a lack of energy, but she was not the type to complain or to overdramatize a health situation. She was stoic about it and not interested in receiving sympathy from others when it wasn't warranted. Austen's mother had been a hypochondriac, so Jane resisted calling special attention to her ailments.

Tomalin reports that in the summer of 1816 Austen was experiencing intense back pains. She was taking on a lot of responsibility in entertaining several of her nieces and nephews, and was trying to complete *Persuasion*, so she was certainly not taking it easy. On July 18 of that summer she completed a draft of *Persuasion*, but she proceeded to rework the text, particularly the final two chapters. Then in March 1817 she acknowledged that the novel was finally complete. (Since it was published posthumously, we don't know if Jane intended for the novel to be called *Persuasion* or if the idea came from Henry or Cassandra.)

By January 1817, Austen insisted that she was feeling better, and wrote that she was "stronger than I was half a year ago." She was able to walk from Chawton into the town of Alton (about a mile away), but she wasn't able to make the return trip. Austen self-diagnosed her illness as rheumatism, and was confident that it was getting better. Indeed, between the months of January and March 1817, in addition to completing revisions on *Persuasion*, she wrote eleven chapters of her final, unfinished work, *Sanditon*. Her will to produce and create was forceful and impressive; however, on the 18<sup>th</sup> of March she had an attack that left her finally unable to write. By mid-April she was bedridden.

The attack was so severe that Austen was encouraged to visit the town of

Winchester (about 15 miles away), where she would receive the best care from capable physicians. She was still writing in letters that she was feeling better, saying she was "low but recovering strength," and continued to demonstrate an outward optimism. However privately, just before her departure to Winchester, she penned her will and testament, and addressed it to Miss Austen—Cassandra was to act as the executor of her will. In Winchester she and Cassandra stayed on College Street at the home of family friends. They arrived in town on May 24th. By July 18th, Jane Austen had left this earth. Her sister Cassandra wrote: "She was the sun of my life, the gilder of every pleasure, the soother of every sorrow, I had not a thought concealed from her, & it is as if I had lost a part of myself."

Jane Austen was buried in Winchester Cathedral. This honor was bestowed on her not because she was a great author, but because her brother Henry had connections in the church. As Tomalin puts it: "It was Henry surely who sought permission for their sister to be buried in the cathedral; splendid as it is, she might have preferred the open churchyard at Steventon or Chawton. But Henry knew the bishop." Her epitaph, carved on the stone covering Austen's grave, speaks about her assets as a human being, but as previously noted, it entirely leaves off the fact that she was an author.

Jane Austen's Epitaph:
In memory of
JANE AUSTEN,
youngest daughter of the late
Revd. GEORGE AUSTEN,
formerly Rector of Steventon in this County.
She departed this Life on the 18th July 1817,
aged 41, after a long illness supported with
the patience and the hopes of a Christian.

The benevolence of her heart,
the sweetness of her temper, and
the extraordinary endowments of her mind
obtained the regard of all who knew her, and
the warmest love of her intimate connections.

Their grief is in proportion to their affection
they know their loss to be irreparable,
but in the deepest affliction they are consoled
by a firm though humble hope that her charity,
devotion, faith and purity have rendered
her soul acceptable in the sight of her
*REDEEMER*.

In the year 1900 Jane Austen's descendants commissioned a brass plaque acknowledging the author's literary contributions and had it installed next to her tomb in Winchester Cathedral. Finally Jane Austen received recognition from her family for her writing. Then in 1929 Austen received an even more important homage from Virginia Woolf in her work entitled *A Room of One's Own*. An ardent feminist, Woolf argues for the importance of Austen's contribution to the lives and letters of women writers, not least in terms of their struggles to achieve autonomy in a male-dominated society. Woolf's praise is in part an acknowledgment that, despite social pressures to conform, Austen refused to be persuaded. Jane Austen knew well that she was a woman writing in a man's world—a patriarchal society that had not yet come to accept and appreciate the intelligence and creativity of the fair sex. Yet Austen ignored the conventions of her society. Woolf states that Austen "wrote as women write, not as men write. Of all the thousand women who wrote novels then, [she] alone entirely ignored the perpetual admonitions of the pedagogue— write this, think that. [She] alone [was] deaf to that persistent voice, now grumbling, now patronizing, now domineering . . . that voice which cannot let women alone." Austen could have married, and she could have had children. But she refused to settle; she refused to fulfill her society's expectations of a woman's proper role and duty because—like Elizabeth Bennett, Fanny Price, and Anne Elliot—she had not yet found true love and refused to compromise. So when there was no Fitzwilliam Darcy or Edmund Bertram or Frederick Wentworth, Jane Austen created them in her imagination. Her six brilliant novels are her offspring. They helped show women how to live life on a woman's own terms, just as Jane had done. And now in the twenty-first century, these novels continue to enlighten women and men to the possibilities that result when mutual respect and true love are achieved in marriage.

This universal message—communicated now to myriad twenty-first-century readers of Austen's fiction and viewers of screen and television adaptations of her works—is perhaps best expressed by the modern-day character Amanda Price in the 2008 British miniseries *Lost in Austen*. Miss Price explains why she identifies with Austen's novels: "I love the love story. I love Elizabeth. I love the manners and the language and the courtesy. It's been part of who I am and what I want. I'm saying . . . that I have standards." Modern-day Miss Price articulates something that is timeless. Therefore, we should all—men and women alike—place flowers at the tomb of Jane Austen for the novels and their message of aiming for true love and mutuality when choosing a life partner.

# Chapter 2

# *Sense and Sensibility*

Jane Austen began her first novel as a teenager in 1795, and the result would eventually be called *Sense and Sensibility*. The working title for her book was *Elinor and Marianne*, and in its first incarnation, Austen scripted the story as a series of letters. This fictional form is known as epistolary, and Austen was following the lead of pioneer English novelists of the eighteenth century, who invented the novel form initially as a series of letters or journal entries—as is the case in Daniel Defoe's *Robinson Crusoe* (1719) and Samuel Richardson's *Clarissa* (1748). Surprisingly, Austen wouldn't produce the final draft of her novel until 1810, some months after she moved to Chawton, Hampshire in 1809. The wide gap between draft and finished product is partly explained by those unproductive years of residence in Bath and Southampton from 1801 to 1809. It wouldn't be until she returned to rural Hampshire that she would be reunited with her novel-writing, revising *Sense and Sensibility* at her table in Chawton Cottage between the years 1809 and 1810. She finally published the novel in 1811.

As in *Persuasion* and *Pride and Prejudice*, a significant part of Austen's plot in *Sense and Sensibility* revolves around the patriarchal legal issue of the entail, a property law conceived during the medieval period intended to keep a family's land intact in the main (and male) line of succession. The law forbade an owner to sell his land. The entail is significant in Austen's novel because it is a law that prevents women from inheriting property—even from their husbands. In this regard, Austen shows her reader the extent to which English society during this period in history was thoroughly sexist, and in a feminist sense, she demonstrates how women must negotiate and survive in such an extreme patriarchal environment. When Mrs. Dashwood's husband Henry dies in the opening of the novel, she and her three daughters, Elinor (age 19), Marianne (age 16), and Margaret (age 13) all become homeless. Mrs. Dashwood is the second wife of Henry Dashwood. Because they have no male offspring, ownership of Henry's estate, Norland Park, by law goes to John Dashwood, son of Henry via Henry's first marriage. In his dying moments, Henry makes John promise to provide financially for Mrs. Dashwood and her daughters; however, John's wife Fanny persuades her husband against providing well for them. Essentially the mother and her three daughters are put out on the street. At one moment they lived in elite luxury as members of the landed gentry, and in the next moment they have nothing and are completely dependent on the kindness of relatives and relations.

Conceiving a plot in which a mother and her three daughters are forced to make their ways in the world without the oversight, guidance, and support of a father or brother allows us to read the novel through the lens of a feminist theme. Keep in mind that Austen's representation of women is not recognizable as modern-day feminism, but it is a precursor. At face value, a woman writing in the early nineteenth century about women surviving on their own without men is a bold and uncommon act. And while her heroines might not be patriarchy-smashing rebels by today's standards, Austen does create women who are smart, strong, and have a great deal of depth. They are not the typically meek, subservient, materialistic women who you would expect to meet on the marriage market of this time period. In Elinor especially, we meet a woman of substance. As the eldest daughter, she acts as the protector of the family. She always places the well-being of others before her own. And where Mrs. Dashwood and Marianne would seem (more typically) to be unhinged at times by emotions, Elinor is able to keep hers in check. We find a connection between the novel's title and its plot when we explore the contrast between these female identities. Elinor is endowed with sense and plenty of it, while Marianne is the emotional one who is connected to sensibility. Some scholars have posited that the relationship between Elinor and Marianne mirrors the one Austen had with her own sister Cassandra. In that configuration, the elder Cassandra had the sense and Jane the sensibility.

Also related to the feminist theme is the extremely precarious position that Marianne and Elinor find themselves in on the marriage market. Both young women are highly attractive, but their values on the marriage market are severely decreased because they are relatively poor—thus Austen teaches us about the extent to which this culture's values are steeped in money and materialism. Austen reminds us that during this time in history, marriage was very much a market, and that more often than not, it was understood as an economic contract—an alliance between families determined to increase land, power, and financial status. Marianne's love interest, Mr. Willoughby, for example, has no immediate fortune, and his rich patron aunt has temporarily cut off his inheritance due to his deviant past behavior. Therefore he must choose between true love (with relative poverty) and no love (with great wealth). Similarly, Elinor has feelings for Edward Ferrars. His problems are somewhat different, but suffice it to say for the moment that his family has also threatened to cut off his inheritance if he fails to marry for wealth and status. In both of these examples we see how marriage is intended to keep money and good breeding in the family.

The fact that the Dashwood women have no money also connects this novel with the theme of social class. The novel introduces us to various levels of social hierarchy. Colonel Brandon, his close friends and neighbors the Middletons, and the John Dashwoods, for example, are all monied members of the landed gentry. Their country estates have been passed down through the generations, and they are connected with an old English country-gentry tradition. Mrs. Dashwood and her daughters are also part of this landed-gentry heritage; however, with the loss of their husband and father, they are entirely cash poor and in dire straits. They will remain so until one or more of the daughters can marry a man with wealth enough to improve their situation. But in spite of these social and economic pressures, we see that Elinor and Marianne both value true love before wealth. As in Austen's other works, true love (not money) is the primary goal in marriage.

With the choice of love or money before many of the characters in the novel, it follows that Austen also presents us with the themes of temptation and greed. Characters like Elinor, Colonel Brandon, and Edward behave with manners that are noble, honorable, generous, selfless, and loving. They are not greedy characters, even when it appears that the circumstances they most desire might be in jeopardy, slipping from their grasps forever. These exemplary characters are rewarded by Austen. In Austen's social vision, good manners and morals count for a great deal. Money and land are not the only measures of elite status in her English society. Decency, honesty, compassion, and sincerity count as well. But some of Austen's characters cannot resist the lure of materialism. And as we will discover, there is a karmic price that they must pay for their greed.

Lastly, in *Sense and Sensibility* Austen is also satirizing the early nineteenth-century construct of the Romantic hero. In many regards, Willoughby fits this role perfectly. He is dashing, introspective, rebellious, and his early actions in the novel are heroic. He would seem to have much in common with Fitzwilliam Darcy of *Pride and Prejudice* fame. But where Darcy becomes more honorable and noble as his exterior layers are peeled away, Willoughby is the opposite. He acts the part of the rake or libertine and ultimately sells out at the end. Austen disguises her villain in a Romantic's clothing. And while we're not sure what to make of Colonel Brandon and Edward Ferrars for much of the novel, Austen surprises us later in the text by representing them as the novel's true, if unlikely, Romantic heroes.

. . .

The first character that Austen represents as an example of greed, selfishness, and snobbery is Fanny Dashwood. Fanny has one son named Harry (who she spoils incessantly) and two brothers, Edward and Robert Ferrars. In this family, Fanny is in control— the domineering wife, mother, and sister. She controls her weak husband, she ensures that his stepmother and stepsisters get none of John's inheritance, and since she detects that her brother Edward has feelings for Elinor, she is immediately motivated to push the Dashwood women out of her social circle and as far away as possible. In her dominance of the people around her, she would seem to be a strong feminine character, but her shallowness, vanity, and greed get in the way of attributing any praise to her.

In contrast to Fanny, the Dashwood women are angelic, and it's not long before they are blessed with a new place to live. A distant relative, Sir John Middleton, has offered the four women the opportunity to reside in a cottage on his property, Barton Park, in Devonshire. Thus, the lion's share of the novel takes place in and around the Middleton's cottage. Accommodations at the cottage in Barton Park are spartan compared with their former lodgings in Norland Park, but the Dashwoods are grateful. Their host, Sir John, is a vivacious, generous, and jubilant man, who is in the habit of throwing parties and enjoying every bit of social engagement that he can. His wife, Lady Middleton, is more reserved and distant than her husband, but Sir John compensates by conspiring with his wife's mother, Mrs. Jennings, at matchmaking, parties, and jovial amusements. Sir

John and Mrs. Jennings are excited by the prospect of locating a match for Marianne (since Elinor is believed to be spoken for by Edward). The most eligible bachelor in the area is Colonel Brandon, a quiet and highly honorable man in his mid-thirties, who is a close friend of the Middletons.

Brandon has a Byronic quality about him—a dark and brooding aspect. The term Byronic is derived from characters created by the Romantic poet Lord Byron. A Byronic character has much in common with the Romantic hero, except the former seems to be in a severe state of suffering, and he is extremely secretive about his past. He stands in opposition to the greed and vanity of his normative society, and there is always speculation that he is guilty of a crime. Colonel Brandon is intensely attracted to Marianne, but unfortunately at the moment the sentiment is not mutual.

Austen contrasts the dark Byronic quality of Brandon with the more classically Romantic appearance of John Willoughby, the nephew of one of the Middletons' neighbors. Willoughby is a handsome and charismatic young man, much closer in age to Marianne than Brandon, and he is filled with all the youthful passion and energy that Marianne seeks. Austen creates Willoughby as the perfect gentleman, and he is possibly even more attractive to women in that, in line with the Romantic hero, he has a tinge of the rebel about him. And the manner in which he and Marianne meet is unparalleled for its Romantic drama. As a Romantic herself, Marianne is a lover of nature and likes to wander the countryside by herself in introspection. On this particular occasion, she is caught unawares by a fierce rainstorm. It strikes so unexpectedly and with such fury that she falls and injures her ankle. Austen has her become a damsel in distress, helpless. Somewhat predictably, and in concert with Austen's Romantic satire, Willoughby shows up on horseback and rescues Marianne, delivering her back home to her stunned mother and sisters.

Over the coming weeks, Willoughby pays daily visits to the Dashwoods' cottage, and initially he can do no wrong. In addition to being attractive and romantic, he proves himself to be highly educated and insightful in the arts. He and Marianne are practically inseparable—reading poetry, laughing, and falling in love. But just as fast as he earned the trust of the Dashwoods and the love of Marianne, in an instant he transitions from Romantic hero to villain. He begins to accomplish this metamorphosis when, during a picnic with the Dashwood family, he and Marianne disappear in his carriage for no explainable reason. Young, unmarried couples were never left unattended during this period in English history. A woman's virtue before marriage could not be called into question; it was the most valuable attribute that she could possess at the altar. Losing her virtue would be scandalous, the ruin not only of the woman in question, but of her entire family. When Willoughby runs off with Marianne, Elinor and Mrs. Dashwood become frightened, and all sorts of questions are raised about Marianne's propriety and honor. Additionally they wonder if Willoughby has proposed to Marianne. When the couple finally returns, it is discovered that they had gone off together to the house of Willoughby's aunt, Mrs. Smith, but Marianne divulges little information to her family about what has occurred.

Even more scandalous is the fact that the very next day, Willoughby makes an early-morning visit to the Dashwood cottage, explains to Marianne that his aunt is sending him off to London on business for as long as a year, and makes a hasty departure. Marianne is hysterical and disbelieving. Over time, to the amazement of all, there is no word from him and no letters forthcoming. Willoughby's heroic status has devolved into that of the antihero. The reader is not yet aware but will soon discover that Willoughby's actions are entirely inspired by economics. In his world, as was most common in Austen's materialistic day and age, money often supersedes love.

While Austen utilizes the trope of the Romantic hero/antihero in her depiction of Willoughby, she employs its antithesis when she invents the character of Edward Ferrars. Shortcomings aside, Willoughby is a classically masculine character, capable of sweeping a woman off her feet and carrying her to the altar. In contrast, Edward appears as somewhat emasculated. Austen proceeds with her Romantic satire when she portrays Edward's propensity to awkwardness. He is indecisive, his thoughts and actions are ambiguous, physically he is clumsy, and at times he stutters when he speaks. His clumsiness is in part explained in that he is in a bind of sorts, but he is only partially forthcoming with the details. Part of his dilemma is that while he prefers the church as a prospective profession, his family disapproves, preferring instead a career in the army or the law for him. The other part of Edward's dilemma is that he has strong feelings for Elinor, but he has been secretly engaged for the past four years to Lucy Steele, a cousin of Lady Middleton. The engagement has been kept a secret because the pair fears that Edward's mother would never approve of the match.

And as for Lucy, she is a character Austen holds up for our ridicule. Lucy claims that her desire for Edward is based on true love, that money doesn't matter, but it's a lie. She is a materialist in a way that is not flattering in Austen's world. For Lucy, like Willoughby, fortune supersedes true love.

As the winter months approach, Marianne and Elinor are resituated in London, where they spend time at the home of Mrs. Jennings. Spending all or part of the winter season in London or Bath was a common experience for young, eligible, and wealthy men and women of Austen's time. The fact was that courting options for men and women were extremely limited outside of cities. And the primary goal of getting young people away from the countryside was to increase their chances of locating an eligible partner. The primary matchmaking event designed for the purpose of uniting prospective couples was the ball.

Upon arrival in London, Marianne still clings to the hope that she will soon to be reunited with Willoughby. She immediately writes to him, then does so again, and again, with no replies forthcoming. When the Dashwood women attend their first ball in town, Marianne finds out why Willoughby has been avoiding her; she discovers that Willoughby is engaged to a woman of high social standing named Miss Sophia Grey. Punctuating Willoughby's materialistic agenda, word comes to Marianne and Elinor that Miss Grey is worth £50,000 (approximately $4,000,000). Indeed the "marriage market" is aptly named. Willoughby's claim to Marianne that he was on business for his aunt in London was partially true; he was hunting for a rich bride, and he found one.

Colonel Brandon becomes a much more significant character at this point in the narrative because he holds the key to understanding Willoughby's strange and unpredictable behavior. Austen accentuates Brandon's Byronic qualities as she has him reveal to Elinor details about his dark, mysterious, and painful past. Brandon was the second son in his landed family. Following the rules of the system of primogeniture, first sons inherited everything, and second sons had to make their own ways in the world—in the military, the professions, or in colonial endeavors. Presumably Brandon has outlived his older brother and therefore, during the time that the novel takes place, he has taken possession of Delaford, his family's landed estate. When growing up, Brandon's father had taken in an orphan girl by the name of Eliza, who was of the same age as Brandon. They fell in love. Brandon equates the passionate feelings they shared for one another with Marianne's feelings for Willoughby. At seventeen, Brandon's father married off Eliza to Brandon's older brother, who cared little for her. Brandon was sick about it and planned an elopement with Eliza, but a servant revealed their plans and they were stopped. Later while Brandon was in the East Indies serving in the army, Eliza and Brandon's brother divorced when Eliza's infidelity was discovered. When Brandon returned from the East, he found her after searching for six months. Sickly, she was in a debtor's prison and died soon after. Brandon tells Elinor that Marianne resembles Eliza, in part explaining Brandon's strong feelings for Marianne. Brandon then relates that Eliza has a three-year-old child, the product of an affair. The child was also named Eliza, and Brandon placed her in school and cared for her. When she was fifteen, she disap-

peared. Brandon eventually discovered that Willoughby had seduced, impregnated, and abandoned her. He had taken her virtue and ruined her for life. Brandon rescued the younger Eliza and placed her and her baby in a safe place in the country.

Presented with the truth about Willoughby, Marianne reacts with incredulity, and her disposition remains dark and brooding. Her response underscores once again the difference between Elinor's sense and Marianne's sensibility. Mrs. Dashwood proposes that they all leave London so as to protect Marianne from the possibility of again running into Willoughby, but plans change when the Dashwoods receive news that Edward will soon be arriving in town. To her credit, Marianne accepts the discomfort she feels and takes joy in the fact that Elinor will have the opportunity to see Edward. As Marianne begins to accept news of Willoughby's new marriage, we do see that she is beginning to recognize and appreciate Brandon.

Before she sees Edward, Elinor has a chance meeting with her stepbrother, John Dashwood. In this exchange, Austen continues to emphasize her society's propensity for petty materialism. John is under the impression that Colonel Brandon has taken an interest in her. Showing this society's obsession with wealth and prestige, Austen has John ask immediately about Brandon's fortune, as if that is the only detail that matters. When he learns that it is substantial, he instructs Elinor about ways she can compensate for her main drawback—her lack of fortune; clearly John is feeling guilty for ignoring his father's death-bed wish to provide for his stepsisters. For Austen, John Dashwood is a another character deserving of ridicule. His obsession with wealth, prestige, rank, and appearances is not to be admired by the Austen reader. We can almost hear Austen scolding John for his shallow, narrow-minded views.

Elaborating on the shallow materialism of her society, Austen has Elinor's conversation with John transition to marriages, or specifically marriages that are engineered or arranged between families for reasons that involve money, power, and prestige. We have already seen how Willoughby's temptation for a wealthy bride superseded his desire for true love. Now Elinor learns that John's brother in-law, Edward Ferrars, may be pushed into an arranged marriage of sorts with a Miss Morton, who John is clear to point out is worth £30,000 (approximately $2,500,000). As a strategy for bribing Edward out of his engagement with Lucy Steele, Edward's mother has offered the prospective couple the sum of £1,000 a year (approximately $80,000) if Edward will consent to the match. Edward wants nothing to do with it. He may be awkward and somewhat emasculated when compared with the hyper-masculine Willoughby, but by resisting these monetary temptations, Austen is showing the superficiality of his family and (by contrast) Edward's substance as an honorable man hoping to marry for true love and not money. Edward has deep feelings for Elinor, but cannot ignore his four-year-old commitment to Lucy. He is also victim to the hostility he feels emanating from his own family about a match with either one of these un-monied women. For the time being he is stuck, ineffective, and ill at ease.

The time soon comes, however, when Edward is forced into action. That is, his family discovers that he is engaged to Lucy Steele. News travels quickly to Mrs. Ferrars, who threatens to disinherit Edward in favor of his younger brother Robert if he does not break off the engagement at once. Mrs. Ferrars' threat is more evidence of the economic climate in which these characters exist. Since Edward is the eldest brother, he, according to the laws of primogeniture, stands to be the primary recipient of his family's inheritance. To forgo that valuable prize for the sake of true love is not an easy decision. Life without money was not a pleasant reality in this materialistic culture. And taking that one step further, Edward is even prepared to forgo both money and love in order to honor his commitment to Lucy. Elinor and Marianne are obviously devastated and even go so far as to call Edward a "second Willoughby"; however, understanding his bind, they have sympathy for the honorable stand Edward is taking in opposition to his family's pressure.

When Colonel Brandon learns about Edward's misfortunes, he too is sympathetic. Edward's situation must remind Brandon of his own struggle between family obligation and the attainment of true love. So much so that Brandon asks Elinor to inform Edward that if he's interested, he could have the clergy position at Delaford (Brandon's estate). The living is modest and not enough to support a family, but Brandon's intention is to help Edward until he is able to improve his situation. Elinor is elated about Brandon's offer. Although many of Austen's characters would look down upon a low-paying clergy position, Elinor (and later Edward) shows her depth of feeling and lack of superficiality and materialism in that she views the option of taking orders and serving the church to be honorable. This makes good sense to the Austen reader when we remember that Austen's father and brother both had rewarding careers as clergymen. When Elinor reports the good news, Edward is ecstatic. Over and over we see what selfless and giving people Elinor and Brandon are, and what an honorable character Edward is.

As winter comes to an end, the Dashwoods get ready to depart from Mrs. Jennings' estate in London and make their way to the cottage at Barton. On their way they plan to stop at Cleveland, the home of Mr. and Mrs. Palmer (Charlotte Palmer is Mrs. Jennings' daughter). When they arrive, Marianne is once again overtaken by her sensibility and state of melan-

choly. She is unable to stop thinking about Willoughby. Now out of the city she is eager to reconnect with
nature, and again, in her Romantic state of mind, she
wanders the pathways and gardens of Cleveland.
She likely wants to recreate aspects of her
isolated walks at Barton when she first met
Willoughby. By the fourth night of their
visit, Marianne comes down with a bad
cold after walking the wet grounds at
twilight. Her condition is poor and de-
teriorates rapidly. She suffers intensely,
struggling with extreme bouts of fever. Elinor and the doctor entertain the possibility that Marianne might not recover from her illness.

Just at the point when Marianne seems
to be taking a turn for the better,
Willoughby shows up in terrible condition;
he is drunk, distraught, and worried
about Marianne. At this crucial stage in
the narrative, Austen is driving home an
important point about personal morality.
Essentially she is telling the reader to be
true to one's own heart, and she reminds
us of the consequences in choosing money
over love. Willoughby has been miserable as a
result of his marriage for money. And beyond his
lack of enthusiasm for his new wife, he is also
wracked by extreme guilt for his abandonment
of Marianne. His ambition is to explain himself to Elinor—to have her understand his
circumstances, so he won't be hated by the
Dashwood women. Over the course of several pages, Willoughby iterates that he truly
loves Marianne, but after his seduction of Miss
Eliza Williams (the ward of Colonel
Brandon, who bore Willoughby

an illegitimate daughter), he was disinherited by his benefactress, Mrs. Smith. Therefore, he justifies his action of abandoning Marianne so that he can be well situated financially by marrying the monied Sophia Grey. Elinor hears him out and has some sense of sympathy. Among other revelations, we discover that Willoughby had not been aloof in London, but rather was obsessively spying on Marianne and Elinor. Willoughby confesses that his marriage was not for love and that he and Sophia Grey are unhappy. He implores Elinor to tell Marianne of his misery and that he has never stopped loving her. Elinor contemplates Willoughby's actions and delivers one of the novel's primary moral messages. To wit:

"The world had made him extravagant and vain— Extravagance and vanity had made him cold-hearted and selfish. Vanity, while seeking its own guilty triumph at the expense of another, had involved him in a real attachment, which extravagance, or at least its offspring, necessity, had required to be sacrificed. Each faulty propensity in leading him to evil, had led him likewise to punishment."

Elinor's assessment of Willoughby is something we might read in a conduct manual. Austen has Elinor criticize not only Willoughby's actions, but also the greedy society that created him.

In *Sense and Sensibility*, we view a marked contrast between characters that behave badly and defy their own hearts, and those characters like Edward and Brandon who struggle to do the right thing. Where Willoughby was a scoundrel, Brandon and Edward are true friends to the Dashwoods, men who do not talk about good deeds, but put them into action. They both provide a true and solid foundational kind of presence in the lives of these women. Brandon has not wavered one bit in his love for Marianne or his devotion to the family—even as he has suffered in his personal life. And likewise, Edward's behavior in honoring his previous commitment to Lucy—even when he is tempted by both his true love for Elinor and the financial arrangement proposed by his mother—is admirable.

Marianne makes a strong recovery from her illness, and acknowledges that she put herself in physical danger as a result of her depression about Willoughby. Her "sensibility" was too extreme. Her understanding of this is accompanied by the realization that she needs to practice and attain the "sense" that Elinor so powerfully possesses and exercises with consistency. Austen positions the relationship between Elinor and Marianne as one between mentor and mentee. While her goals are not what we would recognize as those of modern-day feminists, Marianne is determined to improve herself and strengthen her personal fortitude. Her growing understanding that there is no gain to be had in feeling self-loathing upon a failure of love is a moment of note for women in fiction.

As for Elinor, news arrives about a marriage between "Mr. Ferrars" and Lucy Steele, but Austen has provided us with a twist in the plot: Lucy Steele has married Mr. Robert Ferrars, not Edward! Edward pays a visit to Barton and informs the Miss Dashwoods that his brother (not he) has married Lucy Steele. Elinor's sense, patience, and goodness have finally paid off. Edward explains that he had fallen out of love with Lucy a long time ago, but was simply honoring his previous vow. At the time of his proposal, he had so little knowledge of and experience with women, and he made a "foolish" decision. This fact is born out in that a growing love for Lucy never manifested, and that once Robert became wealthy with the family inheritance, it was Lucy who broke off the engagement to Edward. Clearly Lucy cares more about money than she let on. And now, Edward is free! He proposes to Elinor, and you guessed it— she accepts.

• • •

47

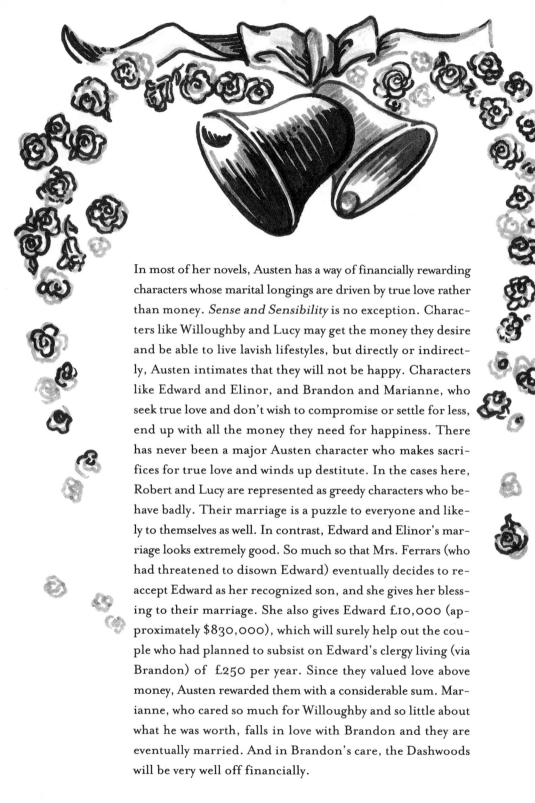

In most of her novels, Austen has a way of financially rewarding characters whose marital longings are driven by true love rather than money. *Sense and Sensibility* is no exception. Characters like Willoughby and Lucy may get the money they desire and be able to live lavish lifestyles, but directly or indirectly, Austen intimates that they will not be happy. Characters like Edward and Elinor, and Brandon and Marianne, who seek true love and don't wish to compromise or settle for less, end up with all the money they need for happiness. There has never been a major Austen character who makes sacrifices for true love and winds up destitute. In the cases here, Robert and Lucy are represented as greedy characters who behave badly. Their marriage is a puzzle to everyone and likely to themselves as well. In contrast, Edward and Elinor's marriage looks extremely good. So much so that Mrs. Ferrars (who had threatened to disown Edward) eventually decides to re-accept Edward as her recognized son, and she gives her blessing to their marriage. She also gives Edward £10,000 (approximately $830,000), which will surely help out the couple who had planned to subsist on Edward's clergy living (via Brandon) of £250 per year. Since they valued love above money, Austen rewarded them with a considerable sum. Marianne, who cared so much for Willoughby and so little about what he was worth, falls in love with Brandon and they are eventually married. And in Brandon's care, the Dashwoods will be very well off financially.

Although her novel has plenty of elements that position it as a contribution to Romantic literature, *Sense and Sensibility* is more accurately a parody or satire of the conventional Romantic plot and characters of her day. The Romantic characteristic of sensibility ultimately proves to be self-destructive. Granted Willoughby makes a good Romantic villain or anti-hero, but Edward and Brandon leave quite a bit to be desired as Romantic heroes.

Romantic literature aside, Austen's novel reveals a great deal about upper-class Regency England and about human nature. The characters in this society are trying to negotiate a strict patriarchy and an obsession with money and status. Austen has some of them give in to temptation, but she balances the greedy and destructive behavior by introducing other characters who are self-sacrificing and who have clear judgment, honorable behavior, and the desire for true love. The attentive Austen reader will recognize many parallels between the world Austen represents to us in her novel and the one in which we live today. Indeed, so many of the challenges faced by Austen's characters have contemporary resonance—and will always have resonance.

Austen's novel has much to say about the resiliency of women. Mrs. Dashwood, Elinor, and Marianne endure trial after tribulation yet they are able to grow and evolve under pressure with grace and fortitude. Austen begins her novel by pulling the carpet out from under the feet of the Dashwood women, stranding them nearly helpless in a dog-eat-dog patriarchal society that is nearly insensitive to their circumstances. What follows from there is like a survival manual. Negotiating one disappointment after another, these women persevere. Austen might agree that unwavering persistence is the key to their survival and their eventual rise to security and happiness. Austen's representation of a stranded single mother and her three daughters determined to make their way is nothing short of a feminist motif that is radical for its day.

Also of crucial importance to the Dashwood women is their unwavering view of and faith in Colonel Brandon and Edward Ferrars. These men have endured a great deal of hardship in their own lives. Like the women who they eventually marry for love, they too have remained constant and persistent in their desires to do the right thing. By contrast, Willoughby and John Dashwood are weak characters. They know they are behaving badly, but they are unable to alter their destinies because they are influenced by greed. Edward and Brandon, however, are good men in this materialistic, patriarchal society, male counterparts to the honorable Dashwood women. Steadfast good behavior is of the highest value in Jane Austen's world. Thus, Austen rewards these men with women who will be lovers, best friends, and true companions for life in a modern-day sense.

# Chapter 3

# Pride and Prejudice

*Pride and Prejudice* is Jane Austen's most popular novel. Her initial draft was called *First Impressions*, and she wrote it during the years 1796 and 1797 when she and her family still resided at Steventon. With the help of her father, she tried to publish it late in 1797, but her work was rejected. She substantially revised the story in 1811 and 1812 when she was living with her sister Cassandra and their mother in the town of Chawton in Hampshire. In 1813 she published the novel successfully in three volumes under its revised title. One of the reasons for the book's blockbuster success during the past twenty years is that it has been represented successfully in several film versions. The BBC production starring Colin Firth (1995) is the most well-respected interpretation, as it attempts to cover nearly all of the novel. Although not as well regarded by the more purist Jane Austen fans, the Hollywood production starring Keira Knightly (2005) has contributed mightily to the novel's popularity.

*Pride and Prejudice* contains themes related to early nineteenth-century social-class issues, economics, and evolving gender identities. Austen introduces us to a combination of landed and middle-class characters who are living in the midst of a changing economy and a changing social order. Great Britain's emerging status as a colonizing empire has created various economic opportunities for members of the middle class. We see rich middle-class characters, who are now eligible to mingle with and even marry members of the gentry. Fifty years earlier, this would not have been possible. Thus, Austen presents us with the gentry of old England (if you will) and emerging middle-class identities that are connected to a new Great Britain. Furthermore, we see a juxtaposition of gentry characters—wealthy and powerful members of the landed gentry and lower-level members, who have much more modest landed estates.

Mr. Fitzwilliam Darcy is a bachelor and landed gentleman who has a great fortune of old money and a regal country estate called Pemberley in Derbyshire. His good friend Charles Bingley is a middle-class character whose family is worth a fortune, but they are without a landed estate. In breeding, Darcy represents old England and Bingley represents the new Great Britain. Darcy is a blue-blood landed gentleman, and Bingley differs in that he is a member of the nouveau riche. He is beneath Darcy in social standing, but he is a representative of the changing British economy, where wealth is now competing with land for status. Likely Bingley has made his fortune abroad in colonial endeavors (although the specific source of his income is not revealed). Like Darcy, Mr. and Mrs. Bennet and their daughters are of landed status, but their estate, called Longbourn, is humble and their monetary income minimal. In the social hierarchy, they are overshadowed by Darcy's estate and fortune of old money, and by Bingley's fortune of new money.

Gender issues are explicitly apparent from the first page as Mr. and Mrs. Bennet have five daughters, each either at or approaching an eligible age for marriage. And as a result of having no sons to inherit the property, a significant portion of the plot revolves around the fate of the Bennet estate. Daughters could not inherit landed property at this time in British history. The Bennets' social status in the gentry allows them to mingle in high social circles, but they are far from what you would call well-monied. This is an important detail as Mr. Bennet is unable to make his daughters more attractive to prospective suitors via extravagant dowries. And since the Bennets have no sons, there is an urgency to find the daughters acceptable partners as soon as possible. As Austen states about Mrs. Bennet, "The business of her life was to get her daughters married."

Two gender issues are extremely important. Firstly, women were eligible on the marriage market for a relatively brief period of time in their lives, from age fifteen until their mid twenties. When a woman reached her late twenties, she was destined for spinsterhood. She would be entirely dependent for her livelihood on parents, brothers, and/or married sisters. There were some employment opportunities for women as teachers or governesses, but options were scarce and hardly desirable. Secondly, outside of visits to London or Bath, opportunities to meet men were minimal for women in these small, provincial communities. A woman could easily fail to meet an eligible bachelor during her courting years, so if she received a proposal of marriage, she was expected to take it no matter what. Love in marriage was not a reasonable expectation for English women during this period in history.

In Austen's world, however, we see women who (like Austen herself) might turn down a proposal of marriage if she was not in love. In *Pride and Prejudice* one of Austen's female characters is willing to risk the tragic consequences if she does not possess loving feelings for her prospective mate. For the time, this was exceedingly radical. We also see male characters who value love in addition to intelligence and freedom of thought in their women— again, a way of thinking that was not commonly accepted in Austen's day.

Finally, the terms pride and prejudice can be interpreted as the trappings of tradition and the patriarchal order in old English society. There is little movement or change in the identities of most of the characters who populate Austen's story. The characters are connected with traditional expectations and ways of thinking about society, marriage, and money. They don't question stereotypical notions of pride and prejudice that are so ingrained and prominent in society. Fitzwilliam Darcy, Elizabeth Bennet, and to a lesser extent Charles Bingley and Jane Bennet all struggle to negotiate the terrain of social pride and prejudice; they evolve and change. Love is what brings them together, and pride and prejudice is what breaks them apart. The work they do in order to overcome social obstacles paves the way for more progressive thinking about marriage, gender roles, and expectations. For this reason at least, Jane Austen is a pioneer for her representations of gender roles and marriage. She is precursor to the modern-day feminist.

As the curtain opens on *Pride and Prejudice*, we meet members of the Bennet family who are central characters in Austen's novel. Mr. Bennet, the patriarch of the family at Longbourn Estate, is bookish and quiet, but he is also honorable, ethical, and extremely wise. His wife compensates for his quietness, as she is like a whirlwind of gossip and idle chatter. The two eldest daughters are Elizabeth (Lizzy), and Jane, followed by Mary, Kitty, and Lydia. With a young woman's urgency to get married in mind, the plot begins as news reaches Longbourn that the rich, eligible bachelor by the name of Charles Bingley has just rented the nearby estate of Netherfield. Remember that Bingley has a fortune, but he is not landed. His wealth, now an acceptable determinant of social value in the new economy of Great Britain, makes him an extremely desirable prize to any of the Bennet daughters. His arrival in the neighborhood creates a massive stir. The call goes out immediately from Mrs. Bennet and all the Bennet girls for Mr. Bennet to pay a visit to Bingley and begin to establish ties.

In fact, Mr. Bennet already has. Going one better, he has arranged for his daughters to attend a ball where Bingley and his entourage (Darcy included) will be in attendance. Bingley is described as "good looking and gentlemanlike [with] a pleasant countenance, and easy, unaffected manners," and Darcy is a "fine, tall person [with] handsome features, [and a] noble mien." We notice that Darcy's description contains an allusion to his nobility ("noble mien"), but the most important detail to observe in the contrasting descriptions is that even though the men are from different social classes, they can bond as equals in friendship because of Bingley's monetary fortune. The upwardly mobile middle class can now compete with the gentry for social positioning.

When the evening of the ball arrives, we see more evidence of just how important social-class issues are in this society. Bingley is the biggest hit at the ball. He is friendly and open, and he seems to take an instant liking to Jane Bennet. Even though he is a man of fortune, he treats everyone at the ball equally with kindness and openness. Darcy, on the other hand, is perceived as cold, aloof, and distant. He is believed to be snobbish and would not dance with any of the young women. Elizabeth is particularly disgusted with Darcy and views him as an elitist. From her perspective, Darcy is embarrassed and annoyed to be in the company of such inferior people, who populate the small and provincial town. Elizabeth perceives that to Darcy, the ball, the townspeople, and the town of Meryton are all socially beneath him.

The distance that Darcy keeps between himself and the members of the ball at Meryton is undoubtedly connected with social-class prejudice. It is not Elizabeth's imagination that Darcy is aloof. But in addition to his snobbery, Austen is fashioning Darcy as a Romantic-hero type, who begins his journey in the narrative as an outsider. The Romantic hero, who was invented as a literary trope or archetype by the likes of Lord Byron and Percy Shelley during the time that Austen is writing, has a dark, mysterious side that he wrestles with. This

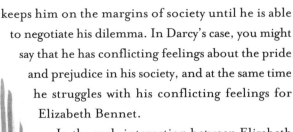

keeps him on the margins of society until he is able to negotiate his dilemma. In Darcy's case, you might say that he has conflicting feelings about the pride and prejudice in his society, and at the same time he struggles with his conflicting feelings for Elizabeth Bennet.

In the early interaction between Elizabeth and Darcy we also see the emergence of Austen's progressive representation of women. Elizabeth understands that as a nobleman, Darcy has his "Pride," and that explains his aloofness in a crowd that he might find to be socially beneath him; however, as Elizabeth states, "I could forgive *his* pride, if he had not mortified *mine*." Elizabeth is a great example of an early fictional female feminist. Her feelings and her dignity are counted— she insists on it. She doesn't play the role of the meek, passive, or subservient female. She has opinions, and she expresses them boldly.

Initially Jane and Bingley are not trapped by the social friction experienced between Elizabeth and Darcy. Since they hit it off at the ball, an arrangement is made whereby Jane should pay a visit to Netherfield to spend time with Charles, his sister Caroline, and his friends. This is all part of Mrs. Bennet's plot to speed up the marital process. Jane, however, becomes ill during her visit, and Elizabeth makes the trek to Netherfield to nurse her sister back to good health. In doing so, Austen continues to develop Elizabeth's character as a liberal female—a tomboy, who walks the three miles to Netherfield. Doing so in the wake of a rainstorm, Elizabeth arrives muddy and receives negative attention for her unladylike appearance. She disregards the protocol, conventions, and manners that are expected of a woman in polite society. Her behavior is nothing out of the ordinary to us in the twenty-first century, but two hundred years ago it would have been scandalous.

Not only is Elizabeth's behavior radical for the time period, but so is Darcy's reaction it. During her time at Netherfield, she is still disgusted with Darcy, but she matches wits with him during the many conversations that take place between the two, so much so that the narrator finally reveals that "Darcy had never been so bewitched by any woman as he was by [Elizabeth]." The implication is that Darcy becomes enamored with Elizabeth because she challenges him with her intelligence. She is able to match wits with him, and he is not put off or threatened. He may not know it yet, but Darcy is an enlightened man because he is attracted to a free-thinking woman.

When Jane is finally nursed back to good health and the party (now including Mrs. Bennet) returns to Longbourn, they are greeted with the news that their cousin, Mr. Collins, will soon be making a visit. This part of the plot involves that British property law the entail (also seen in *Sense and Sensibility*, as we noted, and in Austen's final finished novel, *Persuasion*). The law dictates that landed property cannot be sold and must be retained by the family. Since ownership of land is a means to power and wealth, this medieval law intends that landed estates remain intact. However, emphasizing the degree to which this society is dominated by the patriarch, women were unable to inherit property. Since Mr. Bennet is the only male in his immediate family, none of the females are able to inherit the estate once he has died. When his death occurs, ownership of his property will go to the next closest male relative, in this case the cousin Mr. Collins, a clergyman. He is not close to the family and certainly not well liked, but by law, upon Mr. Bennet's death, Collins will have immediate ownership and could put Mrs. Bennet and her five daughters out on the street.

Mr. Collins is one of Austen's great comical characters. The beginning Austen reader might not expect to laugh out loud when learning about a society of manners, courtship, and proper behavior, but be prepared to enjoy Austen's satire and sarcasm. In the case of Collins, Austen invents him as pompous, awkward, and not easy on the eyes. He is so full of himself, and so clueless in his own ability to assess his personal flaws, that he becomes sad, pathetic, but at the same time riotously funny. We could not laugh at his expense if it were not for his own inflated ego. His patroness is Lady Catherine de Bourgh, a high-ranking member of the gentry, who is a relative of Darcy's. Collins drops her name every chance he gets.

Collins shows up for a visit in part because Lady Catherine encouraged it, but his greater ambition relates to his inheritance of the Longbourn estate. In addition to inheriting the property, he is also keen on inheriting one of the Bennet daughters. In a comical scenario that pokes fun at the courting process (or lack thereof), we see that Collins initially intends to propose marriage to Jane. However, when he discovers that Jane has feelings for Bingley, his sights shift immediately to Elizabeth, and he makes a quick proposal to her. There is no courtship even remotely involved; he pompously assumes that he is a prize and that these women will jump at the chance to accept his proposal. And the sad part is that he is partially right. From a financial perspective, the connection would be extremely helpful to the Bennet family. The estate would stay in the family (as Elizabeth would reside there), and one of the Bennet daughters would be financially taken care of. This arrangement would make Mrs. Bennet exceedingly happy, as one of her five daughters would be taken care of for life. In spite of her mother's wishes, however, Elizabeth cannot accept Mr. Collins's proposal. The prospect of marrying Collins is laughable to her, and it is completely counter to her ambition to marry for love.

Demonstrating his love for Elizabeth, his desire to see her happy, and his respect for her intelligence, Mr. Bennet gives his opinion on the matter in one of the great lines of the novel: "An unhappy alternative is before you, Elizabeth. From this day you must be a stranger to one of your parents.—Your mother will never see you again if you do *not* marry Mr. Collins, and I will never see you again if you *do*." This scene demonstrates Mr. Bennet's qualities as a caring father, who values Elizabeth's future happiness. Indeed, in this regard Mr. Bennet is a free thinker. He is a part of this new society that is progressive in its thinking about the genders and about marriage. Elizabeth's refusal of Collins and her father's reaction to it are pioneering moments for Jane Austen's time. Mrs. Bennet's reaction, however, is connected to old English attitudes about marriage, where love does not factor in the equation.

Also part of the old social order is Collins's next move when he makes another proposal to the family friend and neighbor Charlotte Lucas. Charlotte (like most women of Austen's day) understands that this may be her only chance in life to receive a proposal, and she accepts for practical reasons, not love. Austen presents us with an old social order (in Charlotte) and a new order (in Elizabeth). Since Austen herself was rumored to have declined at least one marriage proposal, we might view Elizabeth's refusal of Collins as somewhat autobiographical.

During Mr. Collins' stay at Longbourn, Elizabeth makes the acquaintance of a Mr. Wickham, a soldier temporarily stationed in nearby Meryton. Social-class issues come back into play as Elizabeth learns that Wickham knows Darcy and that the latter supposedly cheated the former out of a promised inheritance. Being only a soldier was a position in society that would have been held by second and third sons from landed families and

members of the middle class who had no inheritance or fortune to support them. Wickham is resentful of Darcy and clearly feels the sting of class inferiority. Elizabeth is quick to give credence to Wickham's claims, and so we see her feelings for Darcy continue to sour.

As the story within the story goes, Wickham's father had been Mr. Darcy's steward, and when the senior Wickham had passed, Darcy was to have taken care of Wickham financially. Wickham's tale is that he had been raised for a position in the clergy. Darcy was his godfather, and had promised him the living at Rosings Park (now given to Collins). Wickham concludes that Darcy "hates him" and the unfortunate circumstances left Wickham no alternative but to enlist as a soldier. Wickham spends a great deal of energy spreading these rumors hoping to tarnish Darcy's reputation. These allegations fuel Elizabeth's poor opinion of Darcy. Egotistically, Wickham concludes that Darcy acted this way out of jealousy.

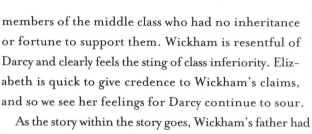

On the heels of Wickham's claims about Darcy's socially superior attitude, the Bennet sisters begin to sense that Darcy and Bingley might be looking down their noses at them. One minute—at a ball thrown by Bingley—Jane is more attached to her host than ever, and there is a clear implication that a proposal of marriage will soon be delivered. As well, Darcy appears to have more substantial romantic feelings for Elizabeth. But in the next instant, Elizabeth receives a puzzling letter from Bingley's sister Caroline stating that the whole group has left Netherfield and gone to

London, and they have no plans to return. The letter states that Charles has business that will detain him indefinitely, and the rest of the group followed to keep him company. There is a hint in the letter that the group looks forward to meeting up with Darcy's sister Georgiana, and that she is intended to be Charles's bride. This news is devastating to Jane, and the Bennet sisters have no alternative but to speculate that to the Bingley's and Darcy's, the Bennet's are not financially or socially adequate.

The following spring, a plan is hatched for Elizabeth to visit Charlotte Lucas and Mr. Collins at their home in Kent, adjoining Rosings Park. While there, Elizabeth visits Darcy's aunt, Lady Catherine de Bourgh, the patroness that Collins earlier could not stop bragging about. Lady Catherine is pretentious and presents herself as stern and intimidating, but in a foreshadowing moment, Elizabeth is not fazed by her. Elizabeth is, however, surprised when Darcy appears unexpectedly, there to visit his aunt.

Unable to contain either her moxie or her pride, Elizabeth continues to stand up to Darcy. Ironically, however, her intelligent wit and cold distancing of Darcy only further kindle his romantic feelings for her. Since Elizabeth is anything but submissive, Darcy's attraction to her shows that he values her stubbornness, her intelligence, and her lack of subservience. A man ahead of his time, he is not looking for a servant, but rather a woman of capability, a partner in the modern sense. But his chances of pleasing her are considerably lessened when Elizabeth learns from Darcy's cousin, a Colonel Fitzwilliam, that it was Darcy all along who influenced Bingley to flee from both Netherfield and Jane Bennet. Furthermore, the colonel confirmed Darcy's low opinion of the Bennet family by unwittingly sharing with Elizabeth that Darcy "lately saved [Bingley] from the inconveniences of a most imprudent marriage."

Not knowing that the conversation between the colonel and Elizabeth had taken place, Darcy pays an abrupt visit to Elizabeth and confesses, "In vain have I struggled. It will not do. My feelings will not be repressed. You must allow me to tell you how ardently I admire and love you." Elizabeth is stunned. As we might expect from a proto-feminist, she confronts him, citing both the influence Darcy had over Bingley to leave Netherfield (and Jane Bennet) and the information she had received about Wickham. On the former count, Darcy doesn't deny the charge about Bingley. Firmly establishing his elite position in the social hierarchy (and confirming Elizabeth's notions about his feelings of social superiority), Austen has Darcy state, "Could you expect me to rejoice in the inferiority of your connections? To congratulate myself on the hope of relations, whose condition in life is so decidedly beneath my own?" With her suspicions about Darcy's arrogance seemingly confirmed, Elizabeth rejects the marriage proposal, and the two separate angrily.

A short time later Elizabeth receives a letter from Darcy that presents his defense. On the matter of Bingley, Darcy elaborates that he believed that Jane did not share Charles' strong feelings, and so he influenced Bingley to spare him from what Darcy anticipated would be a world of heartache. He feels badly about the hurt to Jane, but states that it was "unknowingly done." And as for Wickham, Darcy argues that Wickham ultimately was not fit for taking orders in the church and by Wickham's own admission wished to study law. Darcy assisted him with the amount of £3,000 (worth approximately $250,000), thus settling Darcy's responsibility to Wickham. Wickham, however, did not study law, but was idle. After three years, Wickham returned penniless and demanded that Darcy restore his living in the church as an ordained clergyman (essentially requesting permanent patronage). Not trusting Wickham, Darcy refused, and Wickham responded by attempting to elope with Darcy's sister, Georgiana. The move was economically motivated, as Georgiana's inheritance is worth £30,000 (worth approximately $2,500,000). Wickham's intention was to become rich and gain his revenge through that one act of marriage, but his plot was detected by Darcy before he could carry it out, and ever since, he has been hostile. As his name might suggest, Wickham turns out to be a wicked character, who demonstrates that greed and jealousy are alive and well in this society of manners.

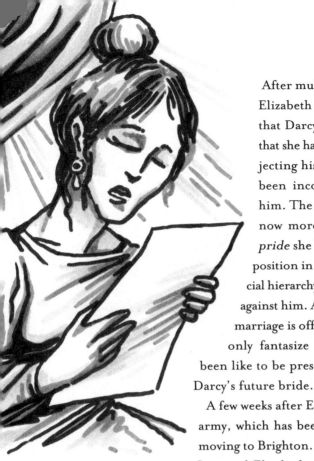

After multiple readings of his letter, Elizabeth comes to the conclusion that Darcy is blameless. She realizes that she has made a huge mistake in rejecting his proposal and that she had been incorrectly prejudiced against him. The meaning of Austen's title is now more apparent than ever. The *pride* she believed Darcy held for his position in society at the head of the social hierarchy caused her to be *prejudiced* against him. And now Darcy's proposal of marriage is off the table, and Elizabeth can only fantasize about what it would have been like to be presented to Lady Catherine as Darcy's future bride.

A few weeks after Elizabeth's return home, the army, which has been stationed in Meryton, is moving to Brighton. Lydia Bennet, little sister of Jane and Elizabeth, had become extremely enamored of the soldiers while they were in town. She desires to follow them, having received an invitation from a Mrs. Foster, wife of the colonel of the regiment. Elizabeth argues against her going, fearing Lydia's "unguarded and imprudent manner," but ultimately Mr. Bennet consents. As we will see, the decision demonstrates inaccurate judgment on the part of Mr. Bennet. Elizabeth's assessment will prove to be the correct one. She may have misjudged Darcy, but Austen shows us that Elizabeth's instincts and intelligence are still highly acute.

Elizabeth gets her next opportunity to travel when she receives an invitation from her relations the Gardiners. Mr. Gardiner is Mrs. Bennet's brother. He is a well-mannered and well-monied businessman, another representative of the growing class of nouveau riche in English society. On their tour of the countryside, they visit Darcy's estate, Pemberley, in Derbyshire, and coincidentally Darcy makes a surprise appearance. Elizabeth is thoroughly embarrassed to have Darcy find her on his estate, but Darcy quickly clarifies that he is happy for the visit and treats

Elizabeth and the Gardiners with extreme cordiality. Reiterating the importance of social class and the place that the possession of money now has in it, Darcy is impressed by the Gardiners' manners and nouveau riche status; he clearly finds them to be more socially acceptable than Elizabeth's mother and sisters.

The enjoyable visit is abruptly cut short when word arrives that Lydia and Wickham left Brighton together and have supposedly eloped to Scotland. Apparently Wickham pursued Lydia romantically while they were both in Brighton. The news is devastating and confirms Elizabeth's earlier belief that Lydia should not have followed the soldiers to Brighton; Elizabeth had been right all along. The family's panic at this development could not be overstated, for Lydia's reputation was not the only one at stake. The marriage-market value of all the daughters would be considerably lessened if Lydia's indiscretion became public knowledge. When Elizabeth tells Darcy what has happened, she feels as if "her power was sinking; every thing *must* sink under such a proof of family weakness, such an assurance of the deepest disgrace." Elizabeth fears that Darcy will avoid her from this time forward as her family's behavior is proving to be even more unacceptable and lower than Darcy had formerly supposed.

66

Mr. Gardiner acts on the family's behalf in searching for Lydia and Wickham. The Bennet family is obviously very tense as they wait for news, but finally they receive a letter from Mr. Gardiner stating that the couple has been found. Apparently they had no intention to marry, but to save face in society, Mr. Gardiner has expressed that if certain minimal financial arrangements are agreed to by Mr. Bennet, that the couple will soon be married. And they are.

When they are delivered back to Longbourn for a visit, Lydia does not apologize for her behavior. Oddly, she does not even seem to acknowledge that she put the reputation of the family in so much jeopardy. To the contrary, she spends her time bragging about being the first married daughter in the family. But then the Bennets learn from Lydia that Darcy had attended their wedding. This detail puzzles Elizabeth, so she questions the Gardiners about Darcy's presence at the ceremony. In Mrs. Gardiner's reply, Elizabeth learns that it was Darcy all along who found the couple and arranged for them to be married. In addition, Darcy intended that these details about his involvement be kept from the Bennet family, hoping instead that Mr. Gardiner would receive the credit. Mrs. Gardiner adds how much she likes Darcy and that he was every bit as nice to them during these last interactions as he had been when they saw him at Pemberley.

In his heroic and noble actions, Darcy would appear to validate the point that social class does matter. At great risk and expense to himself, Darcy acts the part of the hero and modestly wishes no acknowledgment. He does not need to brag, nor does he need to be heralded for his honorable deeds. Austen would probably not deny that heroic actions of this magnitude can only be performed by individuals with

good breeding, excellent manners, and acute intelligence. However, more to the point, Austen intends her audience to understand that Darcy's good deeds are a demonstration of his ardent love for, and devotion to, Elizabeth, in spite of the social-class differences. Love, we should learn, is a more powerful force than social hierarchy, and it can overpower social prejudice. Accordingly, Darcy and Bingley make a return to Meryton, and soon after, Bingley proposes marriage to Jane. Now Elizabeth is certain that she is in love with Darcy, but she doubts they could ever have a chance together after her first refusal.

While Elizabeth ponders her fate, she is visited one morning by Lady Catherine de Bourgh. Here is yet another moment where Elizabeth can demonstrate her powerful female qualities. Lady Catherine informs Elizabeth that she is aware of Jane's recent advantageous marital proposal from Charles, and that she has heard that Elizabeth will soon receive a proposal of marriage from her nephew, Mr. Darcy. This is news to Elizabeth. But Lady Catherine's purpose is to ensure that Elizabeth has no intention of accepting Darcy's proposal. Lady Catherine's reason is that Darcy has been intended to marry her own daughter, Anne de Bourgh. In the English tradition, this would be the acceptable match, as money, alliance, power, and land would be kept in the family. But in Austen's ideal world, people marry for love, not for contractual agreement. Love in marriage has always been Elizabeth's goal, and we see now that it is Darcy's ambition as well. Lady Catherine argues vehemently that Darcy and her daughter are descended from the same nobility, that both their fortunes are extensive, and that they are "destined" to be together. Lady Catherine's diatribe informs Austen's reader that she is firmly part of old-world England, where marriages are contractual and nobility must be preserved at all costs; she is desperate!

In her own most heroic moment, Elizabeth tells Lady Catherine that she cannot be influenced. "You have widely mistaken my character," Elizabeth says, "if you think I can be worked on by such persuasions as these." Lady Catherine leaves deeply angered. The socially inferior Elizabeth has stood up for herself proudly. Indeed, times are changing. Austen shows that there is more to nobility than social rank. Manners, morals, judgment, and intelligence have as much to do with social superiority as anything else.

When Darcy learns the outcome of his aunt's visit, he discovers evidence that Elizabeth still has feelings for him. He makes a quick return to Longbourn and confronts Elizabeth. He tells her that his feelings have not changed, and the two finally become engaged. The couple are a new breed in a new Great Britain. But the material trappings of old England are still so ingrained in this society that the Austen reader cannot entirely dismiss them. When Mr. Bennet learns of Darcy's second proposal and Elizabeth's acceptance, Austen reminds her reader about the value of material in the lives of her characters and the extent to which Austen's world is also so significantly about money. Mr. Bennet says to his daughter, "Oh Lizzy! How rich and how great you will be! What pin-money, what jewels, what carriages you will have! Jane's is nothing to it—nothing at all. I am so pleased—so happy." Mr. Bennet shows his connection to the older generation that believes Elizabeth successful in marriage because of Darcy's social and material worth. But the underlying message—the novel's theme—is that Elizabeth and Darcy are both successful in marriage because (first and foremost) they have found love. The material that comes along with it is certainly important, but to them, we are given to understand, it is secondary.

. . .

The marriages between Jane Bennet and Charles Bingley and Elizabeth Bennet and Fitzwilliam Darcy provide readers not only with a romantic outcome for characters we care deeply about, but they also provide evidence of an English society that is socially and economically in flux. In both marriages, Austen shows us that love supersedes social-class prejudice. Arguably Charles and Jane fall in love the very moment they first meet. Jane's feelings remain constant, but Charles allowed societal prejudice and the degree of difference in their fortunes to influence his feelings. English tradition dictates that social alliances (marriages) should be for land, money, and title first. Love is secondary. During much of the novel, Darcy reminds Bingley that reputation and status matter.

In addition to reinforcing for Bingley the patriarchal standards of old England, Darcy must remind himself that it would be beneath him to marry into a family whose social reputation and standing were far beneath his own. And considering Lydia Bennet's behavior in running off with Wickham, Darcy is provided with no end of evidence that Elizabeth's social standing is beneath his own. Yet, when the last word is written, these two couples will be joined in holy matrimony first and foremost because they are in love.

Austen's understanding and representation of the genders is progressive and pioneering for her time. Darcy, who is arguably the most popular of all of Austen's male characters, is attracted to Elizabeth's intellect. She challenges him and he likes it. Clearly he is not used to this treatment from the majority of women he meets. He falls in love with Elizabeth because he finds in her a companion who is outspoken, free-thinking, and independent. These characteristics were not common or encouraged in women of the late eighteenth century. The invention of an Elizabeth Bennet is evidence that Jane Austen was forward-thinking. Darcy's receptiveness and desire for a smart woman provides evidence that times are changing. In sync with marriages in all of Austen's novels, these couples are friends, lovers, and companions. Pride and prejudice are connected with traditional thinking about marriage. Austen shows the degree to which pride and prejudice are obstacles for these characters. In the end, though, they are not insurmountable.

These marriages may be stepping stones in English society for a more progressive and liberal way of thinking, but we can't ignore the fact that the patriarchal order is still very much in effect. The marriage between Mr. Collins and Charlotte Lucas reminds us that not all women can be cavalier like Elizabeth Bennet (or Jane Austen) and turn down a proposal of marriage. Charlotte is an example of the norm in English society. Her decision is practical. Charlotte is well aware that she might not have another chance at marriage, and the consequences of spinsterhood far outweigh the consequences of a loveless marriage.

Other reminders that the patriarchy is still alive and well include Mr. and Mrs. Bennet. Mrs. Bennet's desperation to see her daughters get married regardless of the match demonstrates the urgency for women in this society to marry. Marriage is a woman's primary goal, and Mrs. Bennet can think of nothing else. Mr. Bennet appears to value his daughter's intelligence and free thinking when Elizabeth refuses Mr. Collins's proposal, but his elation at his daughter's wealth as a result of her marriage to Darcy suggests that for him as well, the criterion of love in marriage is secondary to wealth. That said, we can't scold him too harshly; from his point of view, his modest assets will not begin to support all of his daughters when he is gone. Elizabeth's alliance with someone of Darcy's stature and wealth will ensure that none of his daughters will ever be wanting for material support.

Pemberley represents a middle ground, a hybrid between tradition and the future of England. It functions in the text as a symbol of the progressive love that Elizabeth and Darcy share. Additionally, it represents progressive thinking. In order to achieve their love, both partners have had to shed many layers of pride and prejudice—the trappings of a society so rich in stifling patriarchal tradition. The couple's triumph and union make Pemberley a positive symbol of a new Great Britain. But in the same breath, its grandeur, history, and material value remind us that it is connected with tradition and the landed ancestry of old England.

Finally, the dark conflicts that plagued Darcy and forced him to play the role of the Romantic hero have been resolved. His dark and brooding persona that initially kept him on the margins of society has evolved into that of a well-adjusted gentleman, who is generous, warm, and filled with love. Darcy is a man of feeling and strength, but in the early stages of his interaction with Elizabeth, he was secretly tormented—torn between the desires of his own heart and the desires and responsibilities of his society. The interior struggle he endured is a testament to his drive and desire to be true to himself. Throughout his journey he is often misunderstood, but that is of little consequence to him. His internal battle with the pride and prejudice of his society shows us that he is capable of change. When Elizabeth first meets him, Darcy is incapable of doing right by her because he couldn't reconcile his own feelings. And the same can be said for Elizabeth. But as the couple emerges in union at the end—in spite of the pride and prejudices of their society—the Romantic hero and his heroine have done justice to their own hearts. Having been rejected once, it is no small feat that Darcy is able to propose a second time. It is also impressive that Elizabeth is able to stand up to the likes of Lady Catherine and prove herself as a woman of courage and substance. As a result, we gentle readers can come to no other conclusion but that Darcy and Elizabeth will certainly live happily ever after.

# Chapter 4

# Mansfield Park

*Mansfield Park* is considered to be Austen's least humorous and most complicated and serious novel. The themes she presents are similar to those that appear in her other books: social class issues that involve waxing and waning fortunes, honorable middle-class characters who demonstrate positive social traits, suspect characters from the gentry who show us a contemptible side of England's elite, and a changing of the guard between some members of the middle class and some of the gentry. Taking place between 1783 and 1793, *Mansfield Park* also allows us to look outside of the provincial world of Austen's tiny English communities to catch sight of and access some of the wider world of the late eighteenth century—the aftermath of the American War of Independence (as it is called in Great Britain), the dawn of the Napoleonic Wars, the Industrial Revolution, and the expanding British economy in the colonies. Austen even manages to weave into her plot information about a slave plantation on the island of Antigua. Part of Austen's greatness is that while she is writing about a seemingly small, provincial world in England, the statements she makes about Fanny and the inhabitants of Mansfield Park provide social commentary that transcends the focused stage of the novel's setting. This point about Austen's work in part explains her immense popularity in the late twentieth and early twenty-first centuries. The stories she weaves about her isolated communities are universal and still relevant. We identify with Austen's world on a broad scale and also on a basic human level. No one understands human nature like Jane Austen.

From the first paragraph of the novel, Austen has a keen eye on social class distinctions. The intermingling of social-class stations is achieved when Fanny, the second eldest daughter of Mrs. and Mr. Price of Portsmouth, is sent to Mansfield Park to live with her landed and wealthy aunt and uncle, the Bertrams. This move is intended to take some of the burden off of Fanny's mother Frances, who already has eight children, but most importantly it sets the stage for the novel's great juxtaposition: Austen contrasts poor Fanny's ethics and morals with those of her four elite cousins. We might expect that with such good breeding and privileged upbringing, the Bertram family would be far superior to Fanny in manners and morals; however, this could not be further from the truth. In her depiction of social-class distinctions, Austen demonstrates that in manners, morals, religious faith, and commitment to marrying for love and not rank or wealth, Fanny far outstrips her noble cousins.

In Fanny, Austen creates a character who is steadfast to a fault in her principles. By juxtaposing Fanny with members of the Bertram clan at Mansfield, Austen is able to make the somewhat radical argument that many of the members of England's gentry are immoral, lazy, licentious, disrespectful, unfaithful, and spoiled. In her representation of

Mansfield Park, Austen comes close to arguing that segments of the gentry are rotten to the core. The baronet, Sir Thomas Bertram, wishes to instill strong morals and principles in his children, but son Edmund aside, his efforts are largely failing. The eldest boy Tom has a penchant for drinking and gambling, the eldest daughter Maria is extremely flirtatious and eventually unfaithful to her husband, the youngest Bertram daughter, Julia, elopes with a man who has suspect morals, and Lady Bertram is perpetually lazy, vague, and mentally out of it.

Adding substantially to the coarse behavior at Mansfield Park are the characters Henry and Mary Crawford, who are connected to the area because Mary is sisters with Mrs. Grant (the wife of the current parson at Mansfield Park). As the reader gets to know him, we discover that Henry is a rake, who flirts incessantly with every attractive woman he encounters, including both Bertram sisters and with Fanny. The character of Mary is a bit more complicated. On the one hand, she is a female version of her brother; she has a sharp tongue, is flirtatious, manipulative, materialistic, and shallow. On the other hand, however, Mary can be viewed as a precursor to a feminist personality. She speaks her mind, argues with men, is highly intelligent, and ignores the conventions of a woman's dutiful role in society. In the context of Austen's novel, Mary contributes mightily to the misrule at Mansfield Park. But from a modern point of view, we might reconsider our opinion of Mary Crawford and view her as a strong female.

As an example of misrule among members of the gentry at Mansfield Park, Austen takes a page from Shakespeare and weaves into her text a play within her novel. That is, in the latter portion of Volume I, Sir Thomas is forced to depart from England for many months in order to tend to financial matters at his property on the island of Antigua. While he is away, a friend of Tom's, a Mr. John Yates, arrives on the scene and proposes to the group that for their own amusement they stage a play called *Lovers' Vows*, by Elizabeth Inchbald. To modern audiences, this activity seems rather tame and constructive, but because Inchbald's play is considered risqué and contains flirtatious scenes, its appropriateness is questioned. The play within Austen's novel is significant for three reasons: first, since the misrule occurs when the head of the Mansfield Park household is not present, Austen may be taking a cue from history and drawing a parallel between events at Mansfield and events in Great Britain during the time that she is writing (not the time during which the novel takes place). Since Austen is writing during the Regency period when King George III was largely absent from the throne, Austen might be implying that just as misrule is unleashed at Mansfield Park when the father is away, so misrule is unleashed in the kingdom when its ruler is absent. That is, with no significant role model at the head to provide guidance, moral fortitude is waning and excessive behavior is on the rise. Secondly, the play demonstrates how quickly the characters are willing to participate in an activity that Sir Thomas would disapprove of; even Edmund is seduced into the idea by Mary Crawford. And finally, the play shows us that despite all the temptations and easy opportunities to have a lapse in judgment, Fanny is unyielding in her exemplary behavior. The other characters endlessly insist that she must participate in their production. In spite of extreme peer pressure, however, Fanny resists at every turn. And as a result, she is generously applauded by Sir Thomas when he returns from the West Indies.

Sir Thomas's journey to Antigua is another event in the novel that, small though it may seem, has significant historical and thematic value. Antigua functions as an example of the colonial efforts and opportunism of Great Britain in the Americas and around the world. By the 1780s, Great Britain had long since become dependent on colonial resources. The Triangle Trade, which had begun in the late sixteenth century, would continue into the early nineteenth century. There is much opportunism taking place in the colonial realm, and (as the example demonstrates), landed characters at home in England have become dependent on the colonial realm to sustain their landed estates. We also see here in the late eighteenth century that (in spite of major losses in America) Great Britain is emerging worldwide as a colonizing empire. Thus,  when Sir Thomas departs for Antigua in order to straighten out his affairs because his property is making "poor returns," the reader can assume that the Bertrams are in possession of a sugar plantation that is currently not prospering due perhaps to disruption by the aftermath of the American War of Independence.

In his book *Culture and Imperialism*, the scholar Edward Said is one of the first to discuss the significance of the Bertrams' West Indian property. As Said says, the capital needed to sustain Mansfield Park inside of England is gained outside in the colonial realm. Members of the English gentry can prosper at home in their privileged lifestyles precisely because they are brutalizing and enslaving others outside of England around the world. The critique obviously implicates Jane Austen in the conspiracy that is British imperialism. Value judgments aside, Austen's example of Antigua in *Mansfield Park* is a conduit out of provincial England and into the wider world of European empire-building.

The presence of the British Royal Navy in the pages of *Mansfield Park* also contributes to the thematic content about morals and ethics, in addition to providing a tapestry that ties the novel into an historical context. Since the action takes place in the 1780s, we witness a period in British history where the navy is at an extremely low point in resources, manpower, and morale. We can attribute this primarily to the loss of the war with America. Momentum would not begin to build again until 1793 when the navy gears up to do battle with Revolutionary France in the Napoleonic Wars. Austen has great familiarity with and insight into the British Navy, but that is not surprising when we remember that her two brothers Francis and Charles both had distinguished careers in the navy. Francis, in fact, would eventually reach the position of Admiral of the Fleet (but that's another story).

With Austen's ready knowledge of the ins and outs of naval life, we find how family fortunes wax and wane in concert with naval fortune and misfortune. In *Mansfield Park* we see examples of two very different kinds of naval identity: on the one hand, we see a navy that is downtrodden and depressed. Mr. Price of Portsmouth is disabled and alcoholic, a ne'er-do-well, who is not able to find his way back into naval employment, and who has not amounted to much in or out of naval life. We also see that his son William Price has extreme fears that his career in the navy might be a bust. When we meet him, he is at the rank of midshipman—an introductory position for an officer in training. As William laments when he comes to visit his sister at Mansfield Park, he will be "nothing" if he is not able to get a promotion to lieutenant. Finally we hear about a character called Admiral Crawford, who is the uncle of Mary and Henry Crawford. The Admiral may be a high-ranking member of the navy, but his manners and morals are apparently very low. He has been a terrible influence on his niece and nephew (who we have already learned have extremely bad manners). Fanny and Edmund spend much time contemplating Admiral Crawford's corrupting influence on Henry and Mary. For a considerable portion of the novel, Mary's bad manners are Edmund's greatest regret.

Hinting that brighter days are ahead for the navy, William Price does finally get his promotion from midshipman to lieutenant, and surprisingly it is Admiral Crawford who arranges it. In an apparent changing of the guard, Mr. Price and Admiral Crawford are dark and suspicious characters, but young William is a bright light, full of life and adventure. He represents Britain's and the navy's positive future. Fanny gets to see William in his new lieutenant's uniform as he departs Portsmouth Harbor; the newly minted officer is depicted as dashing, proud, and optimistic.

In spite of all the negativity that resides in the pages of *Mansfield Park*, Austen does see to it that moral and ethical goodness finally win the day. Amidst the moral decay that is emitted by low and high character alike, Fanny and Edmund rise up and finally recognize their mutual love for one another. Edmund fully acknowledges his calling for a career in the clergy, and Fanny fully supports it. Fanny is attracted to substance—no matter the social standing. She has been in love with Edmund practically from the first day she arrived at Mansfield Park. Her devotion has been constant, her faith unwavering. As we have seen, such honorable, steadfast behavior is highly valued in Austen's world. And so Fanny and Edmund will triumph in the end, marry, and live happily ever after. And idealistically, their union will be based on love and not rank or wealth.

. . .

The first paragraph of *Mansfield Park* introduces a tale involving the three Ward sisters, who meet with different fates on the marriage market. The middle sister, Miss Maria, has the good fortune to catch the eye of a baronet, Sir Thomas Bertram, of Mansfield Park. She becomes a lady and lives a life of comfort and security on an English country estate. The eldest sister (unnamed) finds a union with a man who has what Austen considers a most honorable profession: the clergy. She marries the Reverend Mr. Norris, a friend of Sir Thomas Bertram and clergyman at Mansfield Park.

Mrs. Norris will have no great fortune, but she and her husband live in the grand estate's parsonage and are comfortable. Finally there is Miss Frances, the youngest sister, who has no luck on the marriage market and ends up in a middle-class position; she marries an uneducated and unconnected lieutenant of marines, who is one of the poorest characters in any Austen novel. She has not chosen well. Due perhaps to the fact that the novel takes place in the early 1780s (between the war with America and the war with Napoleon's France), Mr. Price's tenure in the navy occurs during a time of relative naval inactivity. As mentioned, his career has been poor, he has no prospects for future success, and he drinks; he also has a temper and, due to a prior injury, walks with a limp.

The disparity between the fortunes of Maria and Frances, coupled with the fact that Sir Thomas isn't able to assist Mr. Price in his naval career, create a rift between Maria and Frances, and for a time, all communication between them ceases. The divide persists for eleven years, until Frances finally writes to Maria requesting help. Mrs. Norris, who finds herself in the middle of the rift, suggests that one child be sent from Portsmouth to Mansfield Park to ease the burden carried by Frances. The goal, according to the Bertrams, is to provide the child with an education and a "proper" introduction to society, so that she might be married without needing lifelong support from her family or relatives. Social class issues, already apparent in the novel, are accentuated when Sir Thomas and Mrs. Norris vow that a distinction should always be clearly demarcated between Fanny and the Bertram children. Fanny is treated perpetually as less than her gentry cousins. In this sense the story has much in common with Cinderella.

Fanny Price makes the journey from the poor, seafaring town of Portsmouth to the country estate of Mansfield Park when she is ten years old. She is two years younger than her cousin Julia, three years younger than Maria. Initially Fanny is lost in the world of Mansfield Park; she is overwhelmed with the immense size of the estate, and she misses her home (especially her brother William) very much. But with time she adapts and takes her backseat role in the family.

Her cousin Edmund is the first to show Fanny kindness; she tells him a little about her family, and he helps her write to her brother William. Edmund is the responsible and ethical son, destined for the clergy. Austen's depiction of this elite family is mainly negative, but Edmund provides us with evidence that the gentry is not all bad. Otherwise the Bertram children—the spoiled and selfish girls, the womanizing, dissolute Tom—are not welcoming to Fanny, treating her more like a servant than a sister.

About five years after Fanny arrives at Mansfield Park, Mr. Norris dies. With his future in the clergy, Edmund should be in line to inherit Mr. Norris' "living," as it is called, but older brother Tom, weighted down heavily by gambling debts, gets his father to sell the living in order to cover the debts. Because the living is a tenured appointment, Edmund will not receive it until the buyer is deceased. We would expect that Sir Thomas could have taken care of Tom's debts without having to sell Edmund's living; however, we discover that there are problems in the colonial realm with the production of sugar in the West Indies. Clearly a large percentage of the family's income is derived from the West Indian source. This information broadens the scope of our knowledge about the emerging British Empire. There's also an irony in that these members of the gentry are experiencing hard times as a result of wasteful behavior, at least on Tom's part.

The situation in the West Indies worsens to the point where Sir Thomas decides to journey to Antigua to straighten out affairs on his plantation.

We don't know a great deal about the problem. As this novel takes place at the close of the eighteenth century, we are still a decade away from the ban on importing slaves to the British colonies (1807) and thirty years from the parliamentary act declaring slave-smuggling in the West Indies an act of piracy punishable by death (1827). Critics speculate that a slave uprising in Antigua could be responsible for Sir Thomas's losses. The exact nature of his "business" is less important than the fact that Austen opens a window for us to speculate about European intervention in the colonial realm.

Sir Thomas takes Tom on the journey with him in hopes that his eldest son will detach himself from negative influences at home and learn some responsibility abroad. Sir Thomas is wary about leaving his family, especially his daughters, as they are maturing, blossoming, and (now at the ages of 20 and 21) continue to be eligible for marriage. He reconciles his concerns with the knowledge that the benefits to Tom are crucial at this worrisome time in his life. What Sir Thomas doesn't anticipate is that affairs in the West Indies require far more attention than expected; therefore, he remains abroad and sends Tom back home by himself.

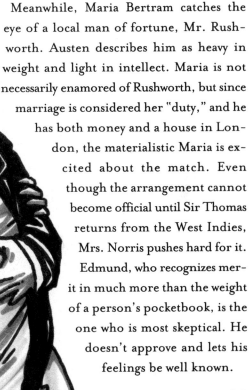

Meanwhile, Maria Bertram catches the eye of a local man of fortune, Mr. Rushworth. Austen describes him as heavy in weight and light in intellect. Maria is not necessarily enamored of Rushworth, but since marriage is considered her "duty," and he has both money and a house in London, the materialistic Maria is excited about the match. Even though the arrangement cannot become official until Sir Thomas returns from the West Indies, Mrs. Norris pushes hard for it. Edmund, who recognizes merit in much more than the weight of a person's pocketbook, is the one who is most skeptical. He doesn't approve and lets his feelings be well known.

The plot is complicated by the arrival in the village of the aforementioned brother and sister, Henry and Mary Crawford. An important detail about the siblings is that they were raised by their uncle, Admiral Crawford. Henry is wealthy, and has since taken possession of his estate in Norfolk. He is described as having a very appealing, charismatic, and flirtatious personality, though he is not handsome. Mary is described as very pretty with a glamorous and scandalous personality. The fact that Henry and Mary have been raised by a high-ranking officer in the navy is an interesting detail in that both brother and sister appear to have been influenced in unsavory ways. In other words, Austen intimates that the salt of the navy has rubbed off on this brother and sister. We don't know a great deal about Admiral Crawford, but Austen does reveal in no uncertain terms that his conduct and his influence on his niece and nephew have been corrupting. One bit of information that we receive is that immediately after his wife passed away, the admiral invited his mistress to live with him. And secondly, Mary demonstrates her uncle's poor influence when she makes a filthy joke to Edmund and Fanny about the navy's "Rears and Vices." The reference (a wordplay on ranks in the admiralty) is to the navy's sordid reputation for the practice of buggery, a most unladylike topic of conversation. As with the representation earlier of Mr. Price of Portsmouth, Austen's depiction of the navy in *Mansfield Park* is predominantly negative. Again, we must remember

that the events here take place well before the great victories that make heroes of naval officers in their defeat of France during the Napoleonic War. We see, for example, a much more heroic depiction of naval officers in Austen's *Persuasion*.

With Mary and Henry now in attendance, and the law of the father (Sir Thomas) in abeyance, the stage is set for a decline in manners and morals and the advancement of misrule. Henry flirts incessantly with both Julia and Maria, and with the latter so much so that she soon believes Henry has serious affections for her. Since Maria is practically engaged, her prospective fiancé, Mr. Rushworth, becomes jealous, uncomfortable, and understandably awkward. Fanny is threatened by Mary's manners, but initially she has Edmund's alliance to keep her company; however, Fanny feels increasingly alone, isolated, and outnumbered when she realizes that Edmund has been blinded to flaws in Mary's character by her good looks. Mary makes an effort to be friendly with Fanny, but generally speaking, Fanny is the odd person out in all of the socializing that takes place. Fanny is an Austen character who reminds us of Elinor in *Sense and Sensibility*. She's never the star, always in the background, always selfless, often forgotten, but she, like Elinor, consistently demonstrates the most honorable behavior.

Letters eventually arrive from Sir Thomas indicating that he has been delayed and will not return home for at least another three months. Mr. Bertram's absence continues to keep the door open for inappropriate behavior. The level of this misbehavior increases when Tom's friend Mr. Yates arrives for a visit to Mansfield Park. And like Tom, Mr. Yates is not an upstanding character. He arrives at Mansfield having just spent time with friends at a theatrical party that was spoiled by the death of a relation to one of the actors. Now he is determined to see the theatrical production through with his new companions.

Inchbald's play *Lovers' Vows* (1798) was frequently staged in London and Bath, where Austen would have had opportunities to view it. Not surprisingly the content of the play involves marital infidelity and illegitimate birth. Along with the risqué subject matter, acting back then (especially for women) was viewed as provocative and potentially scandalous. Times are rapidly changing during the late eighteenth century, yet to a degree actresses are still associated with loose women or prostitutes.

Both Edmund and Fanny instinctively know that Sir Thomas would not condone such a production taking place in his own home, so they initially resist. But, as we have frequently seen up to this point, Edmund is easily influenced by Mary; he changes his mind because he is seduced by the prospect of playing the part of Mary's love interest. Edmund is torn between his morals and his libido, and for the moment, his libido is winning. Fanny is the one who acts according to her senses of decorum and appropriate manners. Even so, she is finally forced to act when Edmund requests it. But just as they are underway, before Fanny delivers a line, Sir Thomas returns, and he is not pleased by what he discovers.

The initial welcome of Sir Thomas is joyous, but since his office had been utilized as the theater space for the production of *Lovers' Vows*, everybody becomes tense when he retreats there. He is angry when he enters to find both Tom and Yates acting out parts of the play. Yates makes an effort to explain to Sir Thomas the evolution of the production, but it has little positive effect. Edmund comes forward to explain that all the young people are to blame excepting Fanny, for she alone resisted the play from the beginning. From that moment on, Edmund's admission endears Fanny to Sir Thomas. This is a new beginning for Fanny, an opportunity to blossom and mature at Mansfield Park with more equal

footing than she has ever known. Apart from his newfound appreciation for Fanny, Sir Thomas is quick to reestablish order in the house for himself and his family. His first task is to see to it that every reminder of *Lovers' Vows* is wiped out of existence. He even goes so far as to burn every copy of the play that he can find. The contrast between life before Sir Thomas' return and after is felt exceedingly by the whole family.

Since Sir Thomas chased all the fun away, Henry and Mary Crawford depart as well. Maria is desperately sad to see Henry leave, as they had been shamelessly flirting during the pre-production of the play. She clearly has passionate feelings for Crawford, but now that he is gone, she is faced with the prospect of marrying Rushworth. Sir Thomas approves of the match and Maria vows not to reveal to Crawford how much his departure has hurt her. The couple is soon married, and a plan is put in motion where Maria and Rushworth venture to Brighton, and Julia accompanies them. The sudden departure of the Bertram daughters creates a significant shift in the family dynamic at Mansfield; Fanny has a much more prominent role in the household and in the parsonage as well, where she spends time with Mrs. Grant and Mary Crawford. Fanny's value has increased. She is still shy, but no longer an afterthought and no longer lurking in corners and shadows.

Eventually Henry Crawford returns to Mansfield, and since Maria is gone, he spends much of his time complimenting Fanny. He even begins to flirt with her! If we had any doubts about Crawford's character, we can now put them to rest; he is a libertine scoundrel who confesses to Mary that he has the intention to make Fanny fall in love with him and then break her heart. Indeed, Crawford is a cruel character, who is much too narcissistic for his own (or anybody else's) good.

In the midst of Crawford's attempted flirtations, Fanny receives news that her beloved brother William will soon pay a visit. William is a midshipman in the Royal Navy, and he is returning from the Mediterranean for a period of leave. Fanny is ecstatic, as she and

William are the closest siblings in their family. When he arrives, William proves to be a superbly mannered young man, and is instantly liked by Sir Thomas and the rest of the family. Through William, Austen makes clear that she has fond feelings for the navy. Sir Thomas often asks William to tell stories about his adventures overseas. When he hears them, even Crawford is impressed and inspired. However, when Crawford begins to feel jealous about William's short but impressive career, one of the novel's main messages comes into focus: the middle-class characters' stock (Fanny and William) is on the rise in society, and the gentry's stock is in decline.

As much as Austen portrays William to be in a desirable position in the navy, the reality is that life on board naval ships was extremely difficult and dangerous. The chances of surviving to the age of 25 during wartime were not good. Diseases of various kinds were responsible for eighty percent of British naval fatalities during the Napoleonic War. In comparison, death suffered at the hands of the enemy comprised only six percent of the toll. Yellow fever, smallpox, typhus, and scurvy were the leading killers, diseases which festered and proliferated because of poor hygienic conditions, poor diet, and cramped quarters. Disease also found its way into the naval community as a result of sanctioned prostitution. Since common sailors were denied shore leave during their tenure in the navy, their only opportunity for heterosexual gratification was with prostitutes who boarded the ship for a time while in port. Naval men-of-war—warships—became floating brothels where disease was rapidly exchanged from shore to ship and ship to shore with devastating consequences.

Adding to these hazards in the naval profession was the fact that in order to make your mark, and in order to make money, a sailor had to have connections and receive a promotion. All officers started out their careers as midshipmen, but if a sailor failed to move up from there, his career would be in ruin. The profession also included a great deal of nepotism. (In *Persuasion*, midshipman Dick Musgrove illustrates the failure to rise up the ranks, while Captain Wentworth's promotion results from his sister being married to Admiral Croft.) Confiding in Fanny, William expresses fear of not being able to get a promotion, called a commission. Fanny and her brother hope initially that Sir Thomas could provide some "influence" that would help William reach the rank of lieutenant. But since Sir Thomas is unable to help, Henry introduces William to Admiral Crawford and the meeting goes well; William will become a lieutenant and act in his new role on board the sloop *H. M. Thrush* (H. M. stands for Her Majesty's).

News of William's promotion is joyously welcomed by Fanny until she learns that everything Henry has done for her brother has been the result of his strong and passionate feelings for her—she is mortified. To make matters worse, Henry declares his love publicly, and Sir Thomas and the rest of the Bertram family are elated. This will mean that Fanny will be taken care of for the rest of her life. She will marry above her social station, and in this world where women are essentially second-class citizens, it would be unheard of for a woman—love or not—to reject such a proposal. But this is Austen's world, where women are free-thinking, and Fanny cannot accept an arranged marriage to a man for whom she has no passionate feeling. Thus, Fanny rejects the proposal and hopes that it would all go away. But it doesn't.

Outraged by Fanny's rejection of the marriage proposal, Sir Thomas tries to convince Fanny to accept it. Part of his strategy is to make Fanny feel guilty for not considering how the arranged marriage would benefit not only herself but her family as well. He deems Fanny selfish, ungrateful, and confused. All the while, Henry attempts to sway Fanny's feelings. She clarifies for him that she considers his actions to be "unsteady." In addition to her strong feelings for Edmund, she has been appalled time and time again by witnessing Henry's flirtations with the Bertram sisters. She cannot trust his wavering actions and moods.

After a long conversation with Fanny, Edmund is satisfied that she has made the correct choice, and he values her for it. Edmund explains his conclusions to his father, in hopes that the family will spend no more time trying to influence and persuade Fanny about her decision. Sir Thomas, however, is still not convinced. He decides that Fanny should make a visit back to her original home in the gritty town of Portsmouth. His thinking is that when she is reunited with her unfortunate economic and social positions, she will come to appreciate the opportunities that a match with Henry will provide. Sir Thomas calls this his "experiment," hoping that a return to her humble former home will "teach" Fanny about the value and importance of money. Here again we see the vital part that economics play in Austen's novels.

Fanny does return to Portsmouth, and initially she is grateful because she gets to see William off to war. Austen's esteem for the navy is apparent as she describes William in his lieutenant's uniform. Fanny is a proud sister. After William's departure, however, we see that Sir Thomas' "experiment" is working; when Fanny first enters her family's rooms, she is appalled because in comparison with Mansfield Park, the place is tiny, dirty, and dark. But we really begin to see Fanny's shock at returning to Portsmouth when she comes to evaluate her interactions with her mother and father. Mrs. Price is called Fanny's "greater disappointment" because she has no love to give to her daughters. Her sons are her pride and joy. Fanny's connection with her father, presented as a mean, crude, boozing, limping, washed-up sailor, is not good either.

When Fanny is enduring her difficult time in Portsmouth, she is surprised by a visit from Henry Crawford. Crawford keeps on coming back. He is determined to convince Fanny of his devotion and steadiness of character. Ironically he seems to have actually fallen in love with her. Fanny is shocked by the visit, and among her other emotions, she feels a sense of shame for the surroundings in which Crawford finds her. When the two are together, they immediately run into Fanny's father. Embarrassed as she is, she is forced to introduce Crawford to him, and to her surprise, Fanny's father behaves in a more respectful manner to this gentleman. In economic terms, Crawford represents relief for the Price family from their depressed economic situation. Henry's efforts in Portsmouth result in an easing of Fanny's negative feelings towards him, but she remains steadfast in her stance not to marry him.

When Henry finally departs for London, Fanny receives a series of troubling letters from Mansfield Park. In the first she learns from Edmund that he is still madly in love with Mary Crawford, and in the next she finds out that Tom is ill. He and his mates got drunk, he took a fall, and now he is seriously ill with fever. Edmund has gone to Newmarket to take care of him. Then Fanny gets an additional shock resulting from a scandal that has reached her father's newspaper. Mr. Price reads that a "Mr. R" (Rushworth) has just lost his wife. It seems that she has run off with a "Mr. C" (Crawford), and nobody knows their whereabouts. Yes, Henry Crawford has shown once and for all that he is not capable of sustained honorable behavior. He is a true-born rake, who has now ruined the reputation of Sir Thomas's daughter Maria.

To round out this rash of disastrous news, Fanny gets another letter from Edmund indicating that now Julia has eloped and run off to Scotland with Yates! Indeed, the Bertram's household has been turned upside down. Since the family is in such disrepair, Edmund implores Fanny to make her return to Mansfield as fast as possible. He also indicates that Sir Thomas has requested that Fanny bring her younger sister Susan with her. The girls leave the next day. Ironically, the Bertrams need Fanny to help restore order to their household. Fanny's stock has increased now more than ever. She has become priceless to her gentry cousins.

In the aftermath of these tragic events, Fanny learns that Mr. Rushworth has been able to procure a divorce from Maria, but Crawford has refused to marry her (leaving the girl in a most disgraceful position). Henry Crawford has ruined his own reputation, which vindicates Fanny. Now she is praised for her ability to resist his advances; and finally Edmund rejects Mary once and for all. In the end (happy for some), Edmund recognizes the value of his cousin and proposes marriage to Fanny. Sir Thomas recognizes that Fanny is the daughter he always wanted, and although he is sad at the prospect of her departure to his son's house, he is comforted by the knowledge that her sister Susan can take Fanny's place as a significant member of the family. Mr. Grant dies shortly after Fanny and Edmund are married, allowing them to move back to the parsonage at Mansfield. Through the strength of her character, Fanny has managed to move up the social hierarchy to become a member of the gentry—by way of marriage.

. . .

From a wide-angle perspective, the significance of *Mansfield Park* is that it allows us to witness not only a family in transition, but also a society in transition. A century earlier, the landed and gentrified Bertram family would have had a much more solid foundation morally and financially. But at the end of the eighteenth century, as depicted by Austen, a family (and country) are in chaos and crisis. Great Britain's imperial colonial activity, the emergence of the Industrial Revolution, and war have all converged to change dramatically the fortunes of landed and middle-class families alike. Since colonial activity (which is fueling the Industrial Revolution) has created opportunities for a multitude of British subjects, social status can now be gained via capitalism, not exclusively by birthright. War too will change fortunes in an instant. Mr. Price of Portsmouth has bad fortune, but his son William will likely fare much better. War, if he survives it, will help him prosper.

And even domestically we see how Fanny's good fortune is gained through the marriage market. Austen is adamant that marriage should not be arranged; title and fortune should not be reasons alone for the package deal. Marriage should be entered into for love. Ironically, however, marriage for love in Austen's world always results in social advantage. The great irony in this novel is that members of the middle class are able to rise in status and cure the ills of a gentry that is having to negotiate major changes in the social fabric of their country. Sir Thomas's visit to Antigua shows us that the gentry is trying to change with the times. But simultaneously, Tom, Henry, and Yates are representatives of a gentry that is lazy, narcissistic, and entirely lacking in ambition. Indeed, in Austen we are witnessing a changing of the guard. Fanny, Edmund, and William are among the new breed of honorable characters that inhabit the gentry; Tom Bertram, John Yates, and Henry Crawford are on their way out.

# Chapter 5

## Emma

Jane Austen wrote *Emma* over a period of fourteen months when she was living a quiet country life in Hampshire with her mother and sister Cassandra. She published her novel in December of 1815, and it would be the last work she would see into publication before her death in July of 1817. On the surface, *Emma* has a great deal in common with other Austen novels in that, as Austen said of all her books, "3 or 4 Families in a Country Village is the very thing to work on." Indeed, *Emma* presents us with a small circle of characters, all of whom live in or visit the small town of Highbury in Hampshire. But upon closer inspection, we discover that in part, the character of Emma Woodhouse is a radical departure for Austen from the kinds of heroines she had been creating up until this point in her career. The major difference: Emma is not interested in marriage.

The theme of marriage is central to all of Austen's novels, and they each include what is called the "marriage plot." This term is used in academic circles to describe domestic novels of the eighteenth and nineteenth centuries that include marriage as the central focus. Marriage is the story's inevitable conclusion, but the audience is usually taken on a roller-coaster ride with the characters as they negotiate obstacles only to eventually find their ways together in union. *Emma* is no exception. However, the interesting question to consider in this marriage plot is: Why is

Emma initially not interested in getting married? When we remember how intricately all of Austen's novels are connected with aspects of economics and social-class hierarchy, the answer becomes clear: unlike the remainder of Austen's heroines who are deeply interested in getting married, Emma is financially well off and therefore does not fathom a reason to get married. As we learn in Austen's novels, marriage is as much an economic arrangement as anything else. Austen's heroines strive for true love, but none is destitute in marriage. Idealistically, they dwell on love and quality of character before financial solvency, but in reality they would make very different decisions if their partners had no wealth. In Emma's case, we know that she has a dowry of £30,000 (approximately $2,500,000). Her money would have been invested in government bonds at a yield of 5%, and thus she would have had an annual income equivalent of $125,000.

As Virginia Woolf might say, Emma Woodhouse has a room of her own and therefore doesn't require a husband to provide one for her. However, we see from the early pages in the novel that other female characters are not so lucky. During this period in history, employment options for women were scarce. If an unmarried woman had no familial source of support, she might find work as a governess or a teacher, but options were not vast. Miss Taylor, for example, had been Emma's governess just before the action of the novel gets underway. She held that position for sixteen years! Having no family money of her own and no father or brothers to support her, she had no alternative (excepting marriage) than to spend so many years of her life in the employ of Mr. Woodhouse. She served in one of the few employment options that were available to women of the early nineteenth century, and she could only give it up when she accepted the marriage proposal of Mr. Weston. This is also the case for Jane Fairfax, the orphan, who is staying in Highbury with her aunt Miss Bates and her grandmother Mrs. Bates. Since the Bates family is in a poor financial situation themselves, Jane has no alternative but to seek a governess position. As Austen demonstrates, Jane is not happy about this unsettling necessity.

The novel makes clear that marriage is essential to the survival of a gentry woman who has no other income. Thus, we witness the positive effects of marriage on the likes of Miss Taylor/Mrs. Weston and Miss Fairfax/Mrs. Churchill. But in addition to showing how marriage can help a woman, Austen also reveals the potential consequences of remaining single. In Miss Bates especially, the reader sees the clear consequences to a woman who fails to marry. Miss Bates had grown up a genteel woman, who was well provided for by her father and brother. Following the death of the males in the family, however, Miss Bates became a spinster. She and her mother live largely upon the kindness and charity of other well-monied members of the Highbury community. Austen draws her as one who the reader pities because of both her lack of wealth, and because of the distasteful aspects of her personality. She is a terrible gossip, other characters that she interacts with seem barely to tolerate her, and she has no ability to gauge when her company is proving tiresome to her audience.

Beyond the dependence women have on money and men in this early nineteenth-century English society, Austen also has a lot to say about how women spend their time. In short, there is simply not a great deal

for women of the gentry to do outside of visiting, socializing, and gossiping. Women of this social class have plenty of servants for all household and child-rearing duties, so this leaves ample time for idleness and social activities. Emma is a perfect example of an intelligent woman, who has too much time on her hands. Aside from looking after her father, the aging Mr. Woodhouse, Emma is entirely free of responsibility. And what she chooses to do throughout the lion's share of the novel is to play at matchmaking. Since Emma has no desire to marry herself, she expends all the energy she might otherwise use for pursuits in that direction on finding a match for her new friend, Harriet Smith. This theme of how a woman of means during this period spends her time is significant. Whether Austen intended to make this point or not, the fact remains that early nineteenth-century women were in the business of killing time. If a woman wasn't obsessed with the goal of marriage, the only option left (Austen appears to be saying) is to play at matchmaking and ensure that someone else will be successful in marriage.

As much as Emma resists marriage, Austen ultimately shows that marrying for true love is the only acceptable outcome. *Emma* teaches that marriage to the right man, in spite of financial independence, should be pursued. And so it is with Emma, who finds her match in the man who has acted the part of her mentor throughout the novel, Mr. Knightly. And as Emma and Harriet Smith, the major characters in the novel, fall in line, the novel reminds us that social and economic hierarchies in society will ultimately be maintained and should not be tampered with. Emma and Knightly are joined in union at the top of the gentry's hierarchy, and Harriet (who is of lower social standing than Emma) and the farmer, Robert Martin, find their union together in the lower-middle class. Emma had been so keen on matching Harriet with Philip Elton, the young and handsome vicar of Highbury; however, she ultimately discovers that the match is not to be.

Social class is also important in *Emma* because here Austen shows the reader a hint of life below the gentry and middle-class positions in society. During this time, at the dawn of the Industrial Revolution, poor people, whose ancestors had been subsistence farmers on medieval estates, are being pushed off the land by Enclosure Acts. These Acts of Parliament, initiated during the late eighteenth and early nineteenth centuries, privatized once public lands and prevented subsistence farmers from being able to freely plant crops and graze animals the way they had for centuries. This produced a sizeable underclass of drifters, many of whom eventually found their ways into cities seeking employment. In *Emma* we see evidence of the underclass when Harriet Smith is accosted for money by a group of "gypsies." The scene provides the reader a window into social class issues we would hardly expect to encounter in a Jane Austen novel. The situation is harrowing for the young woman until Frank Churchill heroically arrives on the scene, saves her, and chases the gypsies away. The presence in the text of the brief encounter with a band of gypsies provides a hint to the reader that not all of England is living like the high-society characters that we find in Austen's novels.

These gypsies remind us that the novel is from a period of history when there is extreme polarity between the rich and poor in society. Additionally there is a reference to a thief who has run off with one of Mr. Weston's chickens. These references are brief and easy to overlook, but they are nonetheless important; Austen's world is not the hermetically sealed paradise that it sometimes seems to be. The outside world—poverty, thievery, the emerging Industrial Revolution—does exist.

Finally, in *Emma*, Austen has created a "comedy of manners." This genre of literature was extremely popular in the Restoration, eighteenth, and nineteenth centuries and was made so by the likes of William Congreve, Richard Sheridan, and Oscar Wilde (among many others). Aside from providing laughs, a comedy tends to bring a community together, and most comedies end in marriage(s). By definition, a comedy of manners is a parody of stereotypes in fashionable society. These comedies (and *Emma* is no exception) often involve love interests, flirtations, and greed, and characters are obsessed with appearances rather than true moral conduct. Although there is ultimately a high standard of moral conduct (created by Knightly among others) that is upheld in *Emma*, there is also quite a bit of shallow and self-consumed behavior that is worthy of critique.

• • •

Emma is the younger of two daughters, and lives in a country estate called Hartfield with her father, Mr. Henry Woodhouse. When Emma was just a child, she lost her mother, and was cared for by a governess named Miss Taylor. When the novel's first page is turned, Emma is twenty years old, and Miss Taylor has recently wed Mr. Weston, leaving (aside from their several servants) Emma and her father to fend for themselves. From

100

the outset we see a marriage between a woman of no means (Miss Taylor) and a man of property (the widower Mr. Weston), who owns a family estate in the area called Randalls (this kind of marital arrangement is common in all of Austen's novels). Mr. Weston, we discover, had been married to a Mrs. Churchill, who passed away. They had a son together named Frank, now 23, and following the death of his mother, Frank was raised under the name of Churchill by his aunt and uncle in London. As we shall see, Frank becomes an increasingly important character in the novel after he initially comes to town to visit his father and his father's new bride. The Westons, Woodhouses, Knightlys, and the Bates family (Miss and Mrs.) are all living in a small provincial area in southern England called Highbury, in Hampshire. Because the marriage between Mr. Weston and Miss Taylor involves a character whose social status greatly increases due to marriage, it foreshadows some of the other love interests and matches that appear later in the novel.

Emma is dedicated to caring for her father, who is a card-carrying hypochondriac. He is allergic to change, and he detests being exposed to the slightest chill. His fussy nature, and Emma's adept strategies for dealing with it, adds significant comic value to the novel. Emma's dutiful qualities are admirable, but less pleasing is the fact that Emma is a spoiled young woman, who is used to having her own way, and who thinks more of herself than is generally healthy.

Another group of characters that often appears consists of Miss Bates, her niece, Miss Jane Fairfax, and Mrs. Bates. Mrs. Bates is a contemporary and friend to Mr. Woodhouse. She is relatively poor. Her granddaughter Jane, who stays with the Bates family, is young, very attractive, and an accomplished piano player. And lastly, Miss Bates, is a pitiable spinster. She's a dedicated friend to Emma, but also very sad, lonely, and gossipy. She provides another example of Austen's comedic wit; however, at times Miss Bates' conversation can be painfully boring. In her thirties, she has little money, no prospects, and as she ages, her situation will likely become worse.

With her dowry in place, however, our heroine Emma, as mentioned, takes a keen interest in playing matchmaker. To prevent Emma from getting into too much trouble, she is repeatedly mentored by her longtime neighbor and brother-in-law, the 37-year-old, most eligible bachelor George Knightly. Of particular concern to Knightly is the way Emma seems to be tampering with the social-class hierarchy. As in all of Austen's novels, the cast of characters includes lower-echelon members of the gentry along with those of the middle class. In her matchmaking, Emma threatens to disrupt and manipulate the existing social order.

The matchmaking aspect of the plot begins when Emma takes credit for the marriage between her former governess and Mr. Weston. Emma is so proud of herself that she thinks she can do the same for her new acquaintance, Harriet. Harriet is an attractive but gullible young woman, who has been educated at a nearby school called Mrs. Goddard's. She has romantic feelings for a successful local farmer, the aforementioned Robert Martin, but Emma convinces Harriet that she can do better (both Harriet and Robert would qualify as members of the lower-middle class, not the gentry).

This is problematic due to the fact that Harriet's parentage is uncertain. She is socially on par with the successful farmer, but Emma leads her to believe that she can attract a man from the gentry.

As a match for Harriet, Emma has in mind the local vicar. Members of the clergy in Austen's time qualify as belonging to the lower echelon of the gentry (along with, as noted earlier, those in the legal profession and officers in the army or navy). Emma doesn't realize it yet, but Philip Elton considers his social status as being far above Harriet's. And part of the parody that Austen weaves through the use of Vicar Elton is that he cares far too much about his social station. In line with a comedy of manners, Elton is more concerned with appearances than he is with his morals and manners. The depiction of Elton has much in common with Mr. Collins of *Pride and Prejudice* fame.

Emma begins her matchmaking strategy by planning activities that involve the three of them. One of the activities is for Emma to paint a portrait of Harriet with Elton in attendance. Emma thinks her matchmaking plan is progressing well, so much so that when Robert Martin proposes marriage to Harriet, Emma makes sure that Harriet refuses. Harriet is like a plaything to Emma, and in this regard, Emma is not sensible. Emma feels the loss of Miss Taylor in her everyday life—this is mainly why she has adopted Harriet as a new friend. But Knightly is not in favor of Emma's meddling. He likes Robert Martin and thinks that he would be a fine and respectable match for Harriet. Emma, on the other hand, scoffs at Martin's credentials for marrying. She belittles Martin for his occupation and lack of education. The social ranks and codes in Austen's society are rigid. Austen has Emma meddle with the social structure, but finally she just succeeds in making a mess of things. Her plan totally backfires when Elton professes his powerful feelings of love for Emma, not Harriet. Elton was under the impression all along that Emma had been flirting with him. As we can imagine, Elton is not going to get over this fast. He's angry and feels as though he has been duped and toyed with. To Emma's satisfaction, he unexpectedly flees to Bath for an indefinite period of time.

From this point, the comedy of manners (or errors, we might say) picks up steam. To begin with, news arrives that during his stay in Bath, Elton has already proposed marriage to Augusta Hawkins, a well-monied woman, who is egotistical, obnoxious, difficult to get along with, and always insists on being the center of attention. Her father is a Bristol merchant, thus we discover that her money is derived from trade and not land and we can locate her in the middle class. When she arrives in Highbury, she continually talks about her life and the people she knows back at home. Elton's extremely quick decision to make a proposal of marriage shows a good deal about his character; his move would seem calculated to get back at Emma. In Elton and his new bride, Austen is continuing to show us how superficial some people in this society can be. Elton appears to have married for both spite and for money.

Meanwhile, Frank Churchill arrives on the scene and impresses everyone in Highbury with his good looks, excellent manners, and thoughtful personality. He is enthusiastic about being a guest in the village. He heartily approves of his new stepmother whom he had never met before, and he showers Emma with a great deal of attention. Emma loves the attention, and for a brief while, she entertains the notion that she might be falling in love with Frank. But finally she dismisses the idea, thinking instead that Harriet and Frank might just make the perfect couple. All plans and flirtations are curtailed, however, when Frank discovers that his aunt's health has taken a turn for the worse, and he is forced to leave abruptly. At first Emma is sad to lose him, but over time her feelings for Frank become less intense. She decides not to encourage his affection.

Some months later Frank returns to Highbury for another visit. Emma worries about how Frank will act with her. She assumes that her "indifference" will have decreased his feeling, and essentially she is right. He is not nearly as attentive to Emma, and spends most of his time either going to or coming from the house of Mrs. Bates. During this visit, there are no emergencies to pull Frank away, so a ball is planned and comes to fruition. That evening, however, there is a most awkward moment when Harriet has no partner. Elton is available to dance, but he refuses to ask Harriet. He shows his true colors as a bitter man. Knightly then rises to the occasion, saving Harriet some awkward embarrassment. Emma is impressed with Knightly's gentlemanly behavior. And when she tells him so, the two of them have a dance together, foreshadowing their future connection. The complication here is that, unbeknownst to Emma, Harriet has now taken a liking to Knightly.

Continuing the comedy of manners, Emma persists in playing matchmaker for Harriet, although after the unfortunate experience with Elton, she plays it sly; she insists to Harriet that she doesn't want to hear any names or have any direct influence. The comedic part is that Emma believes she is playing cupid between Harriet and Frank, when in actuality, Harriet is interested in Knightly. And to fuel the comedy further, Knightly (who is the smartest character in the novel) begins to suspect that there may be something going on between Frank and Jane Fairfax.

Another significant moment in the narrative occurs when all the characters have a picnic at a location called Box Hill. The group is out of sync from the beginning. And adding to the ill feeling, Emma is rude to Miss Bates, insulting her by indirectly stating that her conversation is dull. Although she hides it well, Miss Bates feels the insult most intensely. Later, Knightly scolds Emma for her behavior. We see here and elsewhere

that Knightly mentors Emma, at times praising her for her correct behavior and at other times scolding her for her bad behavior. This kind of mentor/mentee relationship is one that we see often in Austen's novels. Think, for example, of Henry Tilney and Catherine Morland in *Northanger Abbey*, or Edmund and Fanny in *Mansfield Park*.

Next we learn that Mrs. Elton has found a governess position for Jane Fairfax. But before Jane is forced to accept it, Mrs. Weston informs Emma that Frank and Jane Fairfax are engaged. Jane has been saved! Since Frank Churchill possesses old family money and a landed familial estate in Yorkshire, we see yet again an example in Austen's work of different social classes coming together through the bond of marriage. As we know, Jane Fairfax has no money or status in the gentry. She had been forced to find a position as governess and to work for wages. Now, however, she won't have to; her social status is increased dramatically.

As it turns out, Frank and Jane had been engaged since Frank's first visit to Highbury. They had to keep the engagement a secret because Frank knew that his aunt would never approve of the match, as Miss Fairfax's social status is well below their own. Since his aunt has passed away, the couple can now come out in public about their commitment to each other. Emma is sympathetic to Frank and doesn't harbor animosity, but she does feel the weight of having to break the news to Harriet. Remember that Emma thinks Harriet is in love with Frank Churchill. To Emma's surprise, however, Harriet already knows about Jane and Frank, and Emma is doubly surprised to discover that Harriet never had intentions of being with Frank. All along, Harriet tells Emma, she has been in love with Mr. George Knightly! Emma is shocked. Through this information Emma comes to the realization that she too is in love with Knightly and has been so all along.

Emma happily comes to find that Knightly shares her own feelings. The only obstacle in the way of Emma and Knightly being together is Emma's father, who could not live without his daughter and who would refuse to be moved to another residence. But Knightly (the knight in shining armor, so to speak) has already taken this obstacle into consideration; he proposes that he and Emma reside together at Hartfield while Mr. Woodhouse is still living. This is an offer that Emma can't refuse; she, Knightly, and her father will live happily ever after.

The final loose end to tie up is how to break the news of her engagement to Harriet. Emma dreads telling Harriet that she is now engaged to Knightly, because she fears that Harriet still has strong feelings for him. But then Knightly delivers the good news that Robert Martin has just proposed to Harriet a second time, and she has accepted. Harriet, we discover, has always maintained feelings for Robert. We assume that Emma's meddling momentarily confused Harriet, but the correct conclusion is finally realized. Ultimately the social order is reestablished in spite of Emma's tampering. The prosperous farmer is not above or beneath Harriet Smith; the match between them is just right, and the social hierarchy has been maintained.

. . .

Since Jane Austen is so adamant about the need to marry for true love rather than social status or finances, we might think it possible for a Harriet Smith to marry the likes of a Vicar Elton, or a Frank Churchill, or a George Knightly. But since Harriet's parentage is uncertain, and she finds herself somewhere between the middle and lower-middle classes, the gap between her social status and that of a George Knightly is simply too great to overcome. Austen can toy with the idea of such a match (and perhaps like Emma, toy with the possibility of Harriet marrying up such a great distance), but it's not a realistic conclusion. In this sense, we might view Austen as a hypocrite. Marriage, she is saying, should be based on true love, but only when the partners are relatively compatible in social standing.

*Emma* does maintain social-class order, and just as in the other novels, marriages in *Emma* take place between characters that are relatively compatible in their social standing. But different from all the other novels, in *Emma* Austen presents us with a wider spectrum of social-class positions. At the top of the social hierarchy we have the power couple, Emma and George Knightly. Taking into consideration the size of Emma's dowry, and the fact that her fortune will be merging with Knightly's property and fortune, this powerful union in the landed gentry is rivaled in the Austen

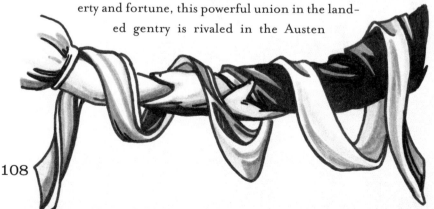

oeuvre only by Fitzwilliam and Elizabeth Darcy of *Pride and Prejudice* fame. Below Emma and Knightly are three marriages that constitute the lower to middling segment of the gentry. Here we have Vicar Philip and Augusta Elton, the Westons, and Frank and Jane Churchill. These marriages are of the scale we are used to seeing in Austen's novels. Similar marriages in other novels include: *Persuasion*'s Anne and Frederick Wentworth, *Mansfield Park*'s Fanny and Edmund Bertram, and *Sense and Sensibility*'s Elinor and Edward Ferrars and Marianne and Colonel Christopher Brandon. All of these characters are from the lower level of the gentry or the upper level of the middle class. In the social-class hierarchy, Harriet Smith's marriage to Robert Martin is the lowest marriage in all of Austen's work. Arguably then, *Emma* contains marriages at both the highest and the lowest levels in any Austen novel.

Well beneath the social-class status quo in *Emma* are the group of gypsies that accost Harriet Smith, and the party(ies) responsible for stealing a bunch of chickens from Mr. Weston's coop. These references are so dramatically outside the realm of Austen's polite social circle that they provide us with a reality check. We can't read these passages without acknowledging that just at the margins of Austen's world (and the margins of the pages in her novels) there are thousands of poor and desperate members of the English underclass, who are stranded in extreme poverty. Austen acknowledges the poor and needy in Emma's (and her own) society when she has Emma and Harriet make a charitable visit to a poor family in Elton's vicarage; however, since Harriet and Emma are so preoccupied with matchmaking and the prospect of seeing Elton, we are left with the feeling that Emma's compassion for the underclasses extends only so far.

109

In addition to the wide spectrum of social-class positions presented in *Emma*, Austen produces a heroine who is arguably her most diverse creation. Simply put, Emma is complicated. From one perspective, she is not a likeable character. In the main, she is egotistical, bossy, manipulative, and at times she lacks patience and empathy. Indeed she is not a typical Austen character. From another perspective, however, Emma may just be Austen's most progressive (dare I say feminist) character. The fact that Emma is not interested in marriage for much of the narrative is significant. In a world where a woman's sole ambition is supposed to be to attract a suitable partner, it is striking and radical that initially she wants no part in a marriage.

Also significant is that this highly intelligent young woman, capable of accomplishments well beyond the imagination of her patriarchal society, is bored sick in her day-to-day existence. She takes up the occupation of matchmaking and she gets herself into trouble because there are no greater challenges that she can pursue. Her charge is to look after her hypochondriac father. Beyond that, her choices are limited. As all upper-class women of the period could attest, their primary occupation (aside from attracting a husband) was killing time by any means necessary. As a woman of the gentry, Emma has no chores to perform and no cooking to do. The undesirable tasks related to her father's care are undoubtedly handled by servants. So aside from socializing with the Westons or the Bates family, Emma takes it upon herself to play at matchmaking. This is her amusement.

Although Emma has a sizeable dowry and is relatively independent, she could not (in a Woolfean sense) have "a room of her own." Her society couldn't envision it. Even Jane Austen lacked a room of her own as she was forced to do all of her writing amidst distractions in the common sitting room. Even so, Emma Woodhouse is an example of a female character in literature who is ahead of her time. You might even say that she has a tinge of the masculine about her. That is, when we describe her as pushy, egotistical, self-centered and the like, we put her down for not acting as a lady of the period should. But aren't these same qualities often respected in a man? Aren't successful men (of any period) often described as stubborn, aggressive, self-centered, hard-charging, and egotistical? Indeed, when Austen wrote *Emma*, she anticipated that her character would not be appreciated the way her other heroines had been up to that point. Her nephew, J. E. Austen-Leigh, reports that upon completion of the novel, Austen had written to a friend that "I am going to take a heroine whom no one but myself will much like." Perhaps we dislike Emma because she is different from other Austen characters that we are used to. She lacks the warmth, softness, and vulnerability of other Austen heroines, such as an Anne Elliot or a Fanny Price. But that shouldn't dissuade us from appreciating Austen's most unusual creation. Emma may not be a successful cupid, but she provides us with another example of a free-thinking woman, who stubbornly goes against the grain of her society. Most readers of *Emma* will appreciate the mentoring that Knightly provides for Emma from time to time throughout the course of the novel. Knightly, we might say, sets Emma straight and guides her behavior to fall in line with expectations and manners of the day. But let us also appreciate the unruly, spoiled, and self-centered Emma, for she, just like the woman who created her, has moxie. She is a precursor for heroines to come whose societies will eventually be able to conceive of a woman's room of her own.

# Chapter 6

*Northanger Abbey*

*Northanger Abbey* is Jane Austen's first completed novel. When she was writing it at the Austen family home in Steventon, both *Pride and Prejudice* and *Sense and Sensibility* were in the works, but *Northanger Abbey* was the first to the finish line. Austen drafted this novel during the years 1798 and 1799 when she was nearing her mid twenties. Ironically, however, it wouldn't be published until late in 1817, after she had passed away. Her brother Henry initially helped her strike a deal with a publisher in 1803, but the book was never printed. Following his sister's death, Henry bought back the book rights and published it elsewhere along with Austen's final novel *Persuasion*.

*Northanger Abbey* is an appropriate beginning for Austen in that it's her least complicated novel. The heroine is a young impressionable girl, who comes of age, and the messages are straightforward and lack the kind of sophistication found in Austen's other five novels. Nonetheless, the work presents us with extremely well-developed characters, who are engaging, funny at times, and thoroughly believable. We see the maturation of Austen's protagonist, and we also see the early brilliance of Austen's use of narration. The narrator here, and in her other novels, does not merely present us with a dry accounting of events; rather, she is like a character in the text. The narrator is sarcastic, bold, opinionated, and at times she even steps out of the story to provide us with significant background information.

We also see a plot that will be repeated throughout all of Austen's other works: Middle-class characters interact with lower-level members of the gentry in English society and increase their social status by way of marriage. As we have discussed so often in these pages, members of the middle class may not have the social pedigree of members of the landed gentry, but their manners and morals sometimes exceed those of their more wealthy counterparts. Additionally, new money-making opportunities are enabling some members of the middle class to compete with the gentry for status in society. In the early and middle portions of the eighteenth century, high society would have consisted exclusively of aristocrats and members of the gentry who had a landed title. Now, in the late eighteenth and early nineteenth centuries, members of the middle class are mingling with gentry figures in high society. We see this in *Northanger Abbey* where Austen has the middle-class Thorpes and Morlands rub elbows with the likes of the Tilneys.

The opening chapters present us with our heroine, Catherine Morland, the fourth of ten children in a family on the cusp between the middle class and the gentry. Her father is a clergyman (the same as Austen's own father), not rich and not poor, and her mother, as we observe by her yield of children, has a "good constitution." As a child, Catherine was a tomboy, who is described as neither beautiful nor intelligent, but at the age of fifteen, "her love of dirt gave way to an inclination for finery, and she grew clean as she grew smart." It was at this age Catherine began training to be a heroine, and thoroughly indulged her love of literature.

When we meet Catherine at seventeen, she is a voracious reader of novels, and has a special passion for Ann Radcliffe's Gothic novel *The Mysteries of Udolpho*. Since the novel is by far the most popular literary form with twenty-first century readers, we may find it hard to believe that in Austen's day the novel (meaning "new") was the least popular and least respected form of literature. In order to confront the negative stigma placed on the novel, Austen's narrator presents her readers with a battle of the sexes—a debate between great English literature of the eighteenth century written by men (Alexander Pope, Laurence Sterne, and Matthew Prior) and less accepted English novels written by women (Frances Burney, Maria Edgeworth, and Ann Radcliffe). Late eighteenth-century England saw a major rise in literature written by women. In particular, women were pioneers of the novel. Women of the late eighteenth and early nineteenth centuries were the primary writers and readers of novels, and distinguished men of letters did not take them seriously. Educated men viewed novels as pulp. To counter the stigma, Austen defends women writers, women readers, and the novel. She has her narrator argue that literature by women is art "in which the greatest powers of the mind are displayed, in which the most thorough knowledge of human nature, the happiest delineation of its varieties, the liveliest effusions of wit and humour are conveyed to the world in the best chosen language." Austen's defense of novels and of the women who write and read them is an early example of feminism. She provides a justification of sorts for her life's ambition in addition to paving the road for her protagonists.

The Gothic novel plays an important role in Catherine's education. She is under a spell of sorts fuelled by her fascination with morbid tales of horror involving murders, terror, dark castles, the supernatural, and most importantly, heroines in distress. Austen knew well the Gothic tradition in literature that spanned the late eighteenth and early nineteenth centuries. As a young girl, Austen shared Catherine's fascination with Gothic tales. And at the forefront of the Gothic tradition in literature was Radcliffe, whose *The Mysteries of Udolpho* (1794) and *The Italian* (1797) were blockbuster bestsellers. In *Northanger Abbey* Austen is celebrating the female author and the Gothic tradition, while at the same time (as we shall see) satirizing her protagonist's innocence and gullibility. Austen is saying that fiction is fun, but it is not reality, and only trouble can come from believing that it is so.

Most of *Northanger Abbey* is set in Bath, a city known not for Gothic edifices but for its Georgian architecture and hot spring, as we have noted. Catherine has the opportunity to make the trip to Bath in the company of Mr. and Mrs. Allen, a wealthy landed couple who own a great deal of property in Wiltshire, the area where the Morlands live. As was commonly the case during the late eighteenth century, Mr. Allen has a medical complaint (in this case gout), and his doctor recommends that he visit Bath for the healing properties that are supposedly contained in the hot water. Since Austen had twice visited relatives in Bath, she knew well the lay of the land.

Upon arrival, the Allen's take Catherine to her first ball at the Assembly Rooms, a magnificent social-gathering place with a large and elegant ballroom. She is overwhelmed by the experience. The English country-dancing, the beautiful rooms with their high vaulted ceilings and chandeliers, and all the well-dressed participants make for a thrilling evening. Unfortunately, though, the Allens don't see anyone they know. As much as she would like to participate in the dancing, Catherine is forced to sit on the sidelines.

Not long after she and the Allens arrive in Bath, Catherine meets a young gentleman named Henry Tilney, whose family belongs to the landed gentry. The couple have their chance encounter at Bath's famous Pump Room, a neoclassical salon where people go to drink the natural hot water and mingle. Tilney, in his mid twenties, is smart and worldly, with hopes of taking orders in the clergy. As a second son, Henry will not inherit his family's fortune—hence his need for a profession. Catherine takes an instant liking to him. They have an engaging conversation about Bath and about keeping journals. Following this initial encounter, however, Catherine doesn't see him again for some time. She hopes to run into him soon, but the opportunity doesn't come.

In Tilney's stead, Catherine meets the Thorpes, whose parents are old friends of Mrs. Allen. Unlike the Tilneys, the Thorpes are of the middle class. Coincidentally, Catherine's older brother James is friends with the Thorpe's son John, and Catherine starts an immediate friendship with the eldest Thorpe daughter, Isabella. Catherine is still missing Henry Tilney, but for the moment she is feeling somewhat better. The two girls share a love of reading, and their first form of bonding is reading Gothic novels together.

When James Morland and John Thorpe arrive in Bath, the foursome begins to spend time together, and John appears to have a crush on Catherine. Expressing her literary interest, Catherine asks John if he has ever read Radcliffe's *The Mysteries of Udolpho*.

117

To Catherine's mortification, John insults the novel, adding cluelessly that if he were to read anything, it would be a work by Ann Radcliffe! When he realizes his blunder, John tries to recover but digs himself in deeper. In spite of his awkward flirtations, Catherine puts up with him because he is both her brother's friend and her friend's brother, but John has not made a positive first impression. He is arrogant and ignorant.

At her second ball, Catherine finally runs into the dashing Henry Tilney, and he introduces her to his sister Eleanor. Ironically Eleanor, who is socially superior, lacks the pretension of the middle-class Isabella and John Thorpe. Austen's description of Eleanor reads like an entry in a conduct manual: Eleanor's "manners showed good sense and good breeding; they were neither shy, nor affectedly open; and she seemed capable of being young, attractive, and at a ball, without wanting to fix the attention of every man near her, and without exaggerated feelings of ecstatic delight or inconceivable vexation on every little trifling occurrence." Eleanor and Henry are members of the gentry who are ethical, honest, and not full of themselves like the Thorpes. This is the social class to which Catherine aspires, but she will have to earn it. The Tilneys have a natural sense of grace, modesty, and sincerity; Catherine is in training.

When Catherine has her next opportunity to meet Eleanor, they have a pleasing conversation and agree that they should see each other the following evening at the cotillion ball. When they meet, Eleanor is with her brother, so Catherine and Henry get another chance to dance and talk. They seem completely charmed by each other. And the added bonus is that Catherine has an opportunity to meet Henry's father, General Tilney, who makes a brief appearance. To top off the evening, she, Eleanor, and Henry decide that they will all go for a country walk the next day. Catherine could not be happier.

As Catherine awaits news from the Tilneys about their country walk, her brother, Isabella, and John Thorpe arrive unexpectedly with plans to visit neighboring Bristol. Catherine initially resists as she is expecting to hear from the Tilneys, but then John mentions a visit to Blaise Castle. This piques Catherine's Gothic interest. Blaise Castle is an important symbol in the text. To Catherine it represents Gothic mystery, the unknown, adventure, and excitement. In her Gothic-fantasy world, Catherine is not merely a plain girl. She is a heroine with purpose on a Romantic adventure. The real Blaise Castle, however, is a "sham castle" built not in medieval times, but in 1766; it's a fake erected entirely for show on a hillside overlooking Bristol. Austen's use of Blaise Castle here foreshadows future Gothic fantasies, and it begins to call our attention to the novel's prominent theme that we should not mistake fiction for reality and truth. Appearances are deceiving.

In order finally to convince Catherine to join them, John lies, telling her that he has just seen Henry in a carriage with an attractive woman heading in another direction. Falling for the lie, Catherine is now convinced that the Tilneys will not show, and accepts the invitation to go on

the outing. Predictably, the day is disappointing. They never reached the promised castle, there was not enough time to visit Bristol, and to make matters much worse, Catherine learned that the Tilneys did come for her after all. What a nightmare (and not of the Gothic variety).

In spite of John Thorpe's continued efforts to keep her away from the Tilneys, Catherine is eventually united with her friends on their country walk. Social-class issues are underscored in the scene, as Catherine gets a tutorial of sorts from Henry. Their conversation covers both practical and erudite topics, including art, history, current events, and differences between the sexes. Demonstrating their elevated social status, the Tilneys are far ahead of Catherine in learning. But Henry acts as a mentor to her, and the walk provides one of many lessons that Catherine receives in her coming-of-age education.

Social class and monetary issues are even more intricately woven into the plot when Catherine learns that Isabella and James have become engaged. Catherine is initially happy about the match, but her view begins to shift when Isabella reveals her monetary agenda. In keeping with Austen's theme that it is important to distinguish between fantasy and reality, Isabella had fantasized that the Morlands were extremely rich, when in fact they are not. In a conversation with Catherine, Isabella waxes about how money is not important to her, that she would be just as happy in a modest cottage as a palace. But there is a disconnect between what Isabella says and what she reveals about herself. In fact, Isabella's statements are false; she is interested in money, and is sincerely disappointed to learn that James will receive only a modest income when he takes orders to be a clergyman. Here is a moment in the novel that connects well with all of Austen's plots: Virtuous characters don't think about money and are therefore often rewarded with income and privilege. Correspondingly, characters who are not favorably depicted (Isabella and John, for instance), and who prioritize wealth are denied. Catherine has no personal income to look forward to, but she does not think of wealth in marriage. She is looking for romantic love.

The last important character to be introduced in the narrative is Henry and Eleanor's elder brother Frederick, an army captain. As the eldest son, Frederick stands to inherit the family estate. In her depiction of Frederick, we see that Austen is not monolithic in her portrayal of social-class status. In other words, she does not create a superficial structure where good characters have education and good breeding and bad characters have the lack. Thus far it might seem that way when we take into consideration that the middle-class Thorpes have lower manners than the Tilneys. When we meet Captain Frederick Tilney, we learn that even landed characters with money, education, and good breeding can also have bad manners. For example, from the moment when he is introduced in the novel, Henry's older brother is inappropriately flirtatious with Isabella. He even dances with her at a ball! Witnessing this behavior is devastating to Catherine, who seems to place the blame more on Frederick than Isabella. Indeed, they are both behaving badly. Catherine feels so sorry and scared for her brother, who, as it happens, is out purchasing Isabella's wedding ring. But this is all part of Catherine's coming-of-age experience. She has seen some of the best qualities in people, and now unfortunately, she has also seen some of the worst.

To that end, Catherine learns that Captain Tilney intends to remain in Bath even after his family has gone back home. Catherine is beginning to see him for what he is— an entitled and spoiled first son behaving like a womanizer and playboy. The news disturbs Catherine, who fears for her brother's well-being. If Frederick and Isabella continue to flirt, their actions will certainly spoil her brother's engagement to Isabella. When she confronts Henry about the situation, imploring him to influence his brother to leave Bath, Henry delivers one of the novel's signature lines: "No man is offended by another man's admiration of the woman he loves; it is the woman only who can make it a torment." Isabella is proving to be extremely cruel. She revels in her flirtations with Captain Tilney, knowing that her fiancé suffers. Henry's poignant lesson to

Catherine on the subjects of flirting and fidelity clarifies that Isabella's behavior is the problem, not Captain Tilney. If Isabella's heart is not constant, James will never be safe. Henry is proving to be a wise mentor for Catherine, and we begin to suspect that he may be testing her. Perhaps he has an ulterior motive.

When her time in Bath has nearly run its course, Catherine receives an invitation from Eleanor to come stay with her family at their country estate called Northanger Abbey. This amazing news ignites Catherine's Gothic imagination. To Catherine the abbey is symbolic. It represents mystery and romance, and it connects with the adventures she has been reading about in Gothic novels. She welcomes the prospect of being scared in the way modern moviegoers welcome the thrill of being frightened at a horror film. But it's more than that for young Catherine. She welcomes having excitement in her life. Dark passageways, secret maps, hidden staircases, frightening characters and the like all present Catherine (and women of the late eighteenth and early nineteenth centuries more generally) with challenges, thrills, excitement, spontaneity, and passion—all aspects of life that were hard to come by for women of the period. Thus, it's no accident that a woman (Ann Radcliffe) was one of the premier and pioneer authors of the Gothic romance and that women were the primary readers of Gothic novels.

During the journey to Northanger Abbey, Austen turns up the heat on her satire of Catherine, who is full of fantasies about the Abbey and beside herself with joy to be driven by Henry.

Understanding Catherine's gullibility and her thirst for Gothic adventures, Henry teases Catherine by inventing stories about dark staircases, secret tunnels, and a mysterious housekeeper named Dorothy—in short, all things Gothic. He describes his home exactly as Catherine imagines it. But when they arrive, Catherine is disappointed to find that the abbey is entirely decorated with modern furniture, and that it could not be further from the Gothic romance she had pictured in her mind's eye. Truth may be stranger than fiction, but Austen continues to warn her heroine that only trouble can come from a failure to be able to distinguish between the two.

Catherine is stubborn, however, and she will not so easily let go of her Gothic fantasy. When she spies an old wooden chest in the room where she is staying, her curiosity gets the better of her. She wonders what it might contain, and hopes that the contents will embroil her in an adventure. But after some secretive effort to find her way into the old chest, she discovers to her great disappointment that it contains merely a well-folded white bedspread; she is embarrassed. That same night a violent storm blows in, complete with lightning and thunder. Catherine welcomes the thrilling atmosphere. Not able to sleep, she looks around the room and spots an old cabinet that she hadn't noticed earlier. She investigates. Being careful not to make any noise, she manages to open the locks on the cabinet doors and discovers many drawers and another locked storage space in the center of the cabinet. She inspects the drawers and finds them empty; however, after working her way into the locked section, she discovers a manuscript. Could this be the clue she has been waiting to find? She is eager to read it before day breaks, but just when she least expects it, her candle is snuffed out and she is lost in total darkness, scared.

She lies awake in bed, eager to inspect the contents of the mysterious manuscript, but when morning comes she finds that it contains nothing Gothic and nothing of interest, just inventory lists of clothing and linens. Once again her great expectations are dashed.

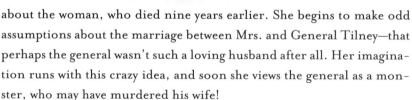

At this point the reader might hope that Catherine would have learned her lesson and understand that no good can come from her obsession with Gothic fantasy, but that is not yet the case. Her hopes of being the central figure in some demonic plot are still alive as she turns her attention towards the deceased Mrs. Tilney. Catherine asks Eleanor about the woman, who died nine years earlier. She begins to make odd assumptions about the marriage between Mrs. and General Tilney—that perhaps the general wasn't such a loving husband after all. Her imagination runs with this crazy idea, and soon she views the general as a monster, who may have murdered his wife!

In order to pursue her hunch, Catherine enters Mrs. Tilney's rooms alone and without permission. She looks around eagerly for clues, but once again discovers nothing out of the ordinary. The rooms hold no evidence of a murder, an imprisonment, or torture. But before Catherine has a chance to exit, Henry discovers her. This time Catherine has gone too far. She confesses to him her suspicions about the general, and he sets her straight. Catherine feels a fool. Additionally, she fears that she has forever lost Henry's trust and friendship. She finally learns her lesson, that novels are romantic and imaginary, but they are not the stuff of reality; the real and the imaginary should remain separate.

Once again we see Henry educating Catherine, acting generously as her mentor as she comes of age. Catherine trusts Henry, and he continues to shape her personality and help her mature. He is a positive influence. He is not spoiled and impetuous like his brother; rather he is smart, handsome, grounded, and highly ethical. He is one of England's finest gentlemen, and Catherine is auditioning to be his wife.

As Catherine begins to feel that she has regained Henry's confidence and trust, she once again thinks about Bath, her friends, and her family members. She receives a letter from her brother James and discovers that he and Isabella have broken off their engagement. James writes that Isabella has made him "miserable forever." Henry and Eleanor are both shocked to hear the news, and they jump to the conclusion that Isabella may now be engaged to Frederick. Soon after, however, Catherine receives a letter from Isabella, stating her dislike for Captain Tilney and imploring Catherine to help her in smoothing things back over with James, whom she hasn't heard from since he left Bath for Oxford. She calls Frederick a "coxcomb," but apparently the reason Isabella is so upset with Frederick is that he has stopped paying attention to her and moved on to a different woman. Catherine concludes from the letter that Isabella is shallow and duplicitous and rejects her plea to contact James.

Catherine and Eleanor then spend a fun week together in the absence of the general who has been forced to leave for London. Henry spends most of the week with the young women, then leaves for a town called Woodston, where he will eventually find his employment as a country curate. Just as Henry departs, the girls get a surprise from an angry General Tilney, who has abruptly returned. Out of the blue he informs Catherine that she must leave Northanger Abbey because the Tilneys have a two-week obligation elsewhere. This means that Catherine is forced the very next day to make a seventy-mile journey back home alone. All of this is so sudden, so disturbing, and so mysterious to Catherine. She wonders if she has angered or offended the general, but departs with no answers. This is as close as she ever gets to participating in a Gothic plot, but it's not the one she was hoping for.

Back at home with her parents in Fullerton, Catherine is confused and extremely sad. She spends most of her time thinking about Henry, hoping that he will not forget her, and she imagines his reaction when he returns from Woodston to discover that she is no longer at the abbey. Two days pass in misery, and her family is concerned about her depressed state. They are not aware of all that has happened to their daughter, and for that matter, neither is Catherine.

On the third day back home, Henry makes a Darcy-like appearance at Catherine's door! She is elated to see him. After introductions to the Morland family, Catherine and Henry go for a walk together, and Henry is able to explain both his own feelings for Catherine and details about what happened back at Northanger Abbey. Firstly, Henry indicates to Catherine that he holds a great deal of affection for her. He relates that during his journey back from Woodston to the abbey, Henry met his father, who informed him that he was never again to see Catherine Morland and that he should immediately break off ties and put her out of mind.

Economic issues foreground the conflict. We discover that John Thorpe's web of lies and deception misled the general about Catherine's social standing. Earlier in the narrative, John (in his most unromantic fashion) had proposed marriage to Catherine via a letter. Although not for an instant seriously considered by Catherine, John felt his proposal would be accepted. Being an accomplished braggart, John told General Tilney that his wife-to-be was worth a fortune. The general believed this about Catherine during the weeks she spent with his family at Northanger Abbey. When he encountered the general again, however, John had already received Catherine's rejection. Knowing that Catherine was visiting with the Tilneys and wanting to hurt her, John revised his account of Catherine's financial situation. This time he told the general that Catherine was destitute; he went overboard again but in the opposite direction. The general's furious reaction to the news reveals his own economic agenda. When the general presents this information to Henry and forbids his son to have any further connections with Catherine, Henry rebels. He is in love with Catherine, and fortune or not, he is determined to propose to her.

This is yet another example in Austen's novels of major characters rebelling against the materialistic conventions of their society and marrying for love, not money. Thus, against his father's wishes, Henry returns to Woodston and then makes the trip to Fullerton to meet with Catherine and express his feelings. Acting the part of the gentleman, Henry asks for and receives permission from Mr. and Mrs. Morland to marry their daughter, but receiving permission from the general would be another matter entirely. Since marriage is a legal contract, permission must be gained on both sides, and the general isn't interested. This obstinacy in the general is indicative of the old guard in England. To him, marriage is an arrangement, a social and economic contract between families to protect and increase land holdings and riches. But a change does occur in the general when Eleanor marries a man of fortune. Demonstrating the influence that money has in this materialistic society, Eleanor demands that the general forgive Henry and let him marry whomever he pleases. Consent is finally gained, and the general's mood about his son and Catherine improves substantially when he learns that, although not rich, Catherine is far from destitute.

. . .

Loose ends are tied, and we are prepared to see these couples living happily ever after. Austen concludes her novel with this provocative final line: "I leave it to be settled by whomsoever it may concern, whether the tendency of this work be altogether to recommend parental tyranny, or reward filial disobedience." "Parental tyranny," as Austen has demonstrated through General Tilney's behavior, is connected with old England, where couples marry for money and power and retain hierarchical status by contracting themselves to members of similar social classes. "Filial disobedience" is in opposition to these antiquated social and economic traditions. Contained in Henry's disobedience to his father is the important theme that love and happiness have value in marriage and should not be forsaken. Henry's actions point the way to new attitudes in a new England, where middle-class characters can mingle with and marry members of the landed gentry, and where love now joins money and social status as an important criterion for evaluating prospective partners on the marriage market.

Also of significant importance is Catherine's refusal of John Thorpe's proposal of marriage. As we have discussed, women weren't in the habit of refusing marriage proposals during this time in history. Yet in Austen's novels, we see it happen in *Northanger Abbey*, in *Mansfield Park*, *Persuasion*, *Pride and Prejudice*, and in Austen's own

life. Austen would seem to be imploring her readers to understand that women have choices. A marriage is a union based on love and compatibility, not a financial contract or a land grant.

Austen's focus on love is a criterion that exists for both women and men. As a second son, Henry Tilney will not be inheriting his family riches or the estate. But he has several options, should he choose them, which can considerably heighten his financial position. As we have seen with Willoughby in *Sense and Sensibility*, for example, Henry could seek out a bride of fortune on the marriage market. Such a move would make him an instant millionaire. This avenue to fortune was extremely common in Austen's day (and to an extent it still is).

And if not through the marriage market, Henry could also have chosen a more lucrative profession, such as business or law. But Henry's choices of both Catherine Morland in marriage and the clergy for his profession demonstrate just how dedicated he is to fulfilling the calling of his heart rather than the calling of his bank account. Austen's heroes and heroines are characters of substance—good role models for each other in the novels and for us gentle readers in our own lives.

In this coming-of-age story, we see Catherine's maturation process as she negotiates the terrain of her society. She has positive role models in the Tilneys and negative role models in the Thorpes. Indeed, *Northanger Abbey* reads like a conduct manual or a how-to book for young women.

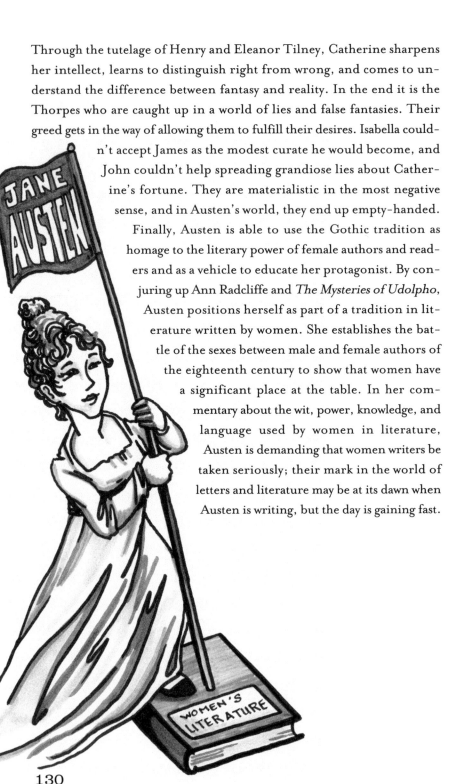

Through the tutelage of Henry and Eleanor Tilney, Catherine sharpens her intellect, learns to distinguish right from wrong, and comes to understand the difference between fantasy and reality. In the end it is the Thorpes who are caught up in a world of lies and false fantasies. Their greed gets in the way of allowing them to fulfill their desires. Isabella couldn't accept James as the modest curate he would become, and John couldn't help spreading grandiose lies about Catherine's fortune. They are materialistic in the most negative sense, and in Austen's world, they end up empty-handed.

Finally, Austen is able to use the Gothic tradition as homage to the literary power of female authors and readers and as a vehicle to educate her protagonist. By conjuring up Ann Radcliffe and *The Mysteries of Udolpho*, Austen positions herself as part of a tradition in literature written by women. She establishes the battle of the sexes between male and female authors of the eighteenth century to show that women have a significant place at the table. In her commentary about the wit, power, knowledge, and language used by women in literature, Austen is demanding that women writers be taken seriously; their mark in the world of letters and literature may be at its dawn when Austen is writing, but the day is gaining fast.

# Chapter 7

# *Persuasion*

*Persuasion* (originally titled *The Elliots*) is Austen's last competed novel, which she wrote during her second-to-last year of life from August 1815 to August 1816. Austen had just completed *Emma* a few months earlier in 1815, and after turning 40, she began feeling poorly, although she wasn't able to identify a specific cause. Since she had grown up with a mother who had hypochondriac tendencies, Austen made a valiant effort to fight through her malaise and avoid complaining. She kept her composure and remained focused on the book until she completed it in July of 1816, but then she wasn't satisfied with her ending. For three more weeks she labored tirelessly over revisions of the final two chapters. Austen would not see *Persuasion* published during her lifetime. She put the novel aside, and in the early months of 1817 began to pen *Sanditon*, a novel that she would never complete. Austen died later that year in July. By December of 1817, her brother Henry wrote a "Biographical Notice of the Author" and included it with publication of a volume that consisted of both *Persuasion* and *Northanger Abbey* (a novel that had not yet been published). No one knows for sure if Austen intended to change the title from *The Elliots* to *Persuasion* or if it was Henry's idea. Of interest is the fact the *Northanger Abbey* is Austen's first completed novel, and *Persuasion* is her last. The novels bookend her career, and they also share the common setting of Bath for significant portions of their plots.

*Persuasion* presents us with more evidence that there is a changing of the guard taking place in British society in the early nineteenth century. As the novel opens, we witness two significant changes taking place simultaneously: the first is that the Napoleonic War has just ended, and British naval officers (most of them from the lower gentry and middle class positions in society) are returning from war victorious. They are heroes, many of them have become exceedingly wealthy off the spoils of war, and now they are looking to settle back on land in private society. Coinciding with the return of these officers is Austen's focus on the Elliots, a family in the gentry who can no longer afford to reside on their familial estate, Kellynch Hall. Due to medieval laws governing the ownership of property, landed estates could not be sold; however, they could be rented.

Sir Walter Elliot, the baronet of Kellynch Hall, represents a segment of titled and entitled England that is dying. Since he has been unable to manage prudently the affairs of his estate, he must "retrench" to Bath in order to downsize his dwelling and reduce the number of servants he and his family rely upon. As he is in need of a tenant who can afford his familial estate, he chooses a naval admiral just returning from war.

Sir Walter is a symbol of vanity, greed, waste, extravagance, and shallowness in early nineteenth-century English society. He is a man who is incapable of taking care of himself or his estate, and he is idle. He cannot do anything other than socialize and find fault in others. In his exceeding superficiality, he looks upon himself as physically handsome and superior to most members of the human race. Accentuating his narcissism and vanity, Austen decorates his rooms with several mirrors, so he can admire himself at every turn. Austen's novel argues that Sir Walter and his kind are on their way out. And in their place are members of the new middle class.

Members of the growing middle class are numerous and varied, but in the case of her novel, Austen is referring specifically to the heroic and newly monied officers of the navy. These men have been serving and protecting Great Britain from the scourge and terror that is Napoleon's France. They are a new breed of gentleman. When they make their return to land, they are welcomed with open arms by a grateful society. And since many of them have made a great deal of money during the war, they can now mingle with the elite in English society. They are invited to the balls in London and Bath, and they are desirable prizes themselves on the marriage market. They may not be landed, but they are loaded. In their earlier days, they went off to war like William Price in the pages of *Mansfield Park*—moneyless, but proud, optimistic, and dashing in their new uniforms. Now Austen manages to capture the precise moment when they return from war with the value of their social stock just soaring. And as they reach land, many of them are looking for brides.

We can contrast this depiction of naval officers in *Persuasion* with depictions of the navy in *Mansfield Park* where Mr. Price and Admiral Crawford are dark and suspicious characters. These depictions are from the time between the wars with America and the Napoleonic War—a time when the navy was in a depressed state. When we contrast the two depictions, we can see how historically accurate Austen's representation of the navy is, drawing on her knowledge of the naval life gleaned from her two brothers' successful careers. When Fanny Price sees William off to war looking smashing in his new uniform, we can sense that brighter days are ahead for the navy. Now in *Persuasion*, that vision is realized.

The light and dark representations of naval officers that Austen provides in *Persuasion* and *Mansfield Park* are also connected to the tropes of the Romantic and Byronic heroes that were conceived during Austen's lifetime by Romantic authors such as Lord Byron and Percy Shelley. By definition the Romantic hero is a character on the margins of society—an outsider. The alienated and introspective hero fights to triumph over the forces that separate him from the mainstream. Captain Frederick Wentworth is an example of the Romantic hero type. Before his luck in war, he was, according to Austen, a "nobody." He was barred admittance into polite social circles. However, in the end he triumphs and is able to transcend that social divide.

The Byronic hero type (a term that refers to characters created by Lord Byron) differs from the Romantic hero in that these characters are more significantly flawed. The Byronic hero is suffering from some unnamed secret sin in his past. He is darker than the Romantic hero and potentially not redeemable. He has the quality of the bad boy or troublemaker about him. In Mr. Price and Admiral Crawford of *Mansfield Park*,

Austen provides more than a hint of Byronic qualities. Even Wentworth may have a tinge of the Byronic persona about him, especially when we read between the lines.

But Frederick Wentworth is redeemable, and the key ingredient that assists in his redemption is money. Money now has a more commanding voice in British society, and as a result, landed members of the gentry are interacting with sailors. Over the course of the preceding century, there had been a great deal of opportunism talking place in the colonial domain. We see this in *Mansfield Park* as Sir Thomas is in possession of a sugar plantation on the island of Antigua. War too—or victory in war—has created opportunities for many of these sailors. They may lack the landed status of the gentry, but due to the significant rise of capitalism, colonial opportunism, and the increasing importance of money, these sailors, who at one time were shunned by polite society, are now welcomed guests.

Among those eager to welcome the victorious sailors back home are the Musgroves, a country-gentry family connected to the Elliots through Sir Walter Elliot's youngest daughter Mary, who is married to Charles

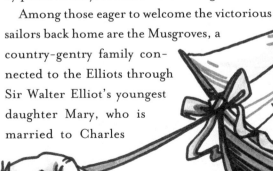

Musgrove. Although landed, the Musgroves are not a refined family. They lack both the sophistication and the condescension of the Elliots. Charles is very likable, but Mary is a hypochondriac to an extreme degree. She complains of various ailments to the point where she becomes a comedic character. Charles also has two sisters, Louisa, nineteen, and Henrietta, twenty. They are both attractive and figure into the plot as prospective partners for the dashing Captain Wentworth.

When we investigate the title *Persuasion*, the social-class issues begin to come clearly into focus. The background is as follows: Eight years before the present-day action of the novel, sailor Frederick Wentworth came to visit his brother, who lived near Kellynch Hall. Having some interactions with the Elliot family, the sailor fell in love with, and proposed marriage to, Anne Elliot. Anne was in love with Wentworth, and if she could have had her own way, she would have accepted his proposal. The problem, however (and here is where the title comes in), was that Anne was persuaded by a family friend, Lady Russell, to turn down Wentworth's proposal. Wentworth was just starting out in his career. He was not wealthy, he was not of the gentry's status, he didn't have great prospects, and as a sailor, he worked in a most "uncertain" profession. Lady Russell, along with the rest of the Elliot clan, rejected the idea. Feeling like there was no other option, Anne acceded to the wishes of family and friends'.

This connection between Wentworth and Anne eight years earlier allows Austen to provide her readers with a great deal of information about the navy and the uncertain aspects of the profession. We see how important nepotism is, for example, in getting a promotion. Wentworth received his promotion due to the fact that his sister, Sophia, was married to Admiral Croft. And because a promotion was essential in putting Captain Wentworth in a position to make money during the war, he could not have done so well for himself without the family connection. Naval officers were able to earn what is called "prize money" in wartime by sacking enemy ships. The background here is that sailors received certain amounts of money by the naval administration for the value of prizes (ships) captured. As a reward to the captain of the capturing vessel and the members of his crew, they received incentive pay for defeating enemy ships, and taking enemy prisoners. All crew members received a portion of the prize money; however, captains got the lion's share. All of this history exists as background in the pages of Austen's novel. In fact, when Wentworth arrives on the scene in the early chapters of *Persuasion*, the reader discovers that he has just been "paid off," a term used by the navy when an officer receives his prize money. This pay transforms Wentworth into a desirable prize himself on the marriage market, as war has made him into a millionaire.

As we discover in all of Austen's novels, her protagonists—in this case the character Anne Elliot—function as precursors of feminist characters. Although she appears for much of the novel as a Cinderella figure, Anne is no exception. She is thoughtful, smart, and compassionate—a woman of substance, who is not bedazzled by riches and status. She differs from, say, Emma Woodhouse or Elizabeth Bennet in that she doesn't impose her will on others in society. In Anne's case, society's will (or more specifically Lady Russell's) is imposed on her. Anne looks back to the decision she failed to get right eight years earlier. However, where most of the women in the novel are entirely dependent on men, Anne is capable of acting and caring for others in a way that is not commonly seen. Anne has compassion for her impoverished, ailing former school friend Mrs. Smith, she never complains, and is not vain like her sister Elizabeth. Anne is very much alone through the pages of the novel, but she never disappears. And at moments when there are crisis situations to be dealt with, Anne rises to the occasion. She keeps her head, manages the situations, and finds resolutions. Ultimately she is valued for her resolve and is finally noticed for her selflessness. In the end, she is rewarded.

In addition to the nascent feminist depiction of her protagonist, Austen also presents us with Sophia Croft, who is Wentworth's married sister. During a dinner party at the Musgroves, we discover that on numerous occasions Sophia has accompanied her husband Admiral Croft to sea. When Sophia relates stories about her adventurous travels with her husband, Austen shows us a woman independent, fearless, full of adventure, and a partner (not a dependent) for her husband. Sophia's experiences provide an extremely positive example for Anne.

The most significant way that Sophia influences Anne is that she married the admiral for love, not for status or money. In concert with each of Austen's major novels, marriage for money and status is looked down upon, but marriage for love is the prize. Anne was persuaded eight years earlier to reject Wentworth's proposal of marriage because his value on the marriage market wasn't adequate. For Lady Russell, the fact that Anne was in love with Wentworth had no bearing on the decision. Love was superfluous—a plus if the suitor was rich and landed, but by no means the priority. Now Austen, through the character of Sophia Croft, is emphasizing to her reader that marriage for love is the priority—the key ingredient that must be present in order for the couple to coexist successfully. And now Anne is lucky enough to get a second chance.

• • •

The year is 1814, the Napoleonic War has just ended, and officers of the victorious Royal British Navy are returning home. Some of them have become wealthy through the incentive system of naval prize money. Such was the case for both Admiral Croft and Captain Wentworth (Austen notes that Wentworth is now worth £25,000, which translates in modern-day U.S. currency to $2,500,000). Austen depicts Wentworth as handsome, honorable, heroic, and a most eligible bachelor. In tune with his brother-in-law Frederick, Croft is heroic, a loving husband, and a jovial man with a witty sense of humor. Hence we find them all together, because Croft, a native of Somersetshire, desires to return with his wife to his old stomping ground. He rents a country estate from the baronet, Sir Walter Elliot.

Austen opens the novel with vain, pretentious, and wasteful Sir Walter Elliot, who when we meet him is admiring his name in a Who's Who collection listing the many baronets of England. The 54–year-old gentleman is selfish and shallow, thinking more of his physical appearance than anything else. He has three daughters: the vain, mean, and self-consumed Elizabeth, hypochondriac and pathetic Mary, and our heroine Anne, who is sweet, shy, routinely wounded by her father and sister Elizabeth, honorable, generous, and good. We discover in the first chapter that Sir Walter's late wife, Lady Elliot, had adeptly managed household affairs, but since her loss thirteen years earlier, Sir Walter has made a mess of the family finances. And we witness early on the social-class climbing of naval officers, who are well monied, in need of places to live, and can afford a country estate. In contrast we see the removal of improvident members of the gentry, who must relocate because they can no longer afford their grandiose homes and extravagant lifestyles. Sir Walter's lawyer suggests that the family relocate to Bath, where they can enjoy a life of luxury at reduced cost.

Anne is the character who links the Elliot family to the sailors, in particular Captain Wentworth. Since rejecting Wentworth's proposal of marriage eight years earlier, she has never ceased loving him. In fact, Anne, now 27 and quickly approaching eternal spinsterhood, was the first choice for marriage to Charles Musgrove but rejected him because of feelings she still harbored for the captain. Charles in turn married Anne's sister Mary. Now that Wentworth is back on the scene, life for Anne has become awkward and uncomfortable. Wentworth remembers the way he was spurned and wants nothing to do with Anne. And to make matters worse for our heroine, Wentworth is fawned over by every unmarried girl who sees him.

As Sir Walter and Elizabeth depart for Bath, and Admiral Croft and his wife move in to replace them, the Elliots' plan is that Anne will visit her sister Mary at the Musgrove estate and join her father and sister later in Bath. As a result, Anne is forced to spend much uncomfortable time watching Charles Musgroves' sisters Louisa and Henrietta (the latter engaged to a country curate named Charles Hayter) flirt shamelessly with Wentworth. Anne is understandably depressed, but endures the difficult situation with grace. This in spite of the fact that the entire Musgrove family is impressed with Wentworth for his looks, heroism, eligibility as a bachelor, and pocketbook. Even Charles is awestruck by Wentworth! The Musgrove brother and sisters are happy to welcome Wentworth to the neighborhood, and for some days they all spend time together walking the countryside, hunting, and socializing. During all these social visits, Anne is like a shadow. She feels like an outsider and tries to cope as well as she can, but she's not the object of anyone's attention.

After receiving a letter of invitation from a sailor friend of his, Captain Harville, Wentworth talks the group into visiting the coastal town of Lyme, where some of his navy friends are living. Captain Harville is another heroic sailor, but he differs from Wentworth in that he had been injured in war leaving him lame, and he was not financially lucky in war. Due to these hardships, he appears much older than Wentworth even though the men are approximately the same age. He and his family live humbly in this seaside town. Captain Benwick is also with them. He was lucky financially in the war but unlucky in marriage; he is presently mourning the loss of his wife, Captain Harville's sister.

This contrast between lucky and unlucky captains provides the reader with a telling depiction about just how uncertain and tenuous the naval profession was during that period in British history. Wentworth had been "lucky" in his profession. This is not to say that he wasn't a capable leader and officer, but still, he was lucky to have connections in the navy that allowed him to move up in rank, lucky to gain command of good ships, and lucky to see action that proved to be financially lucrative. Prize money functioned as an incentive during wartime, but distribution could be anything but fair. As history bears out, captains were well aware that enemy merchant vessels were worth a great deal more in the prize system than enemy warships. This is not to say that Wentworth was guilty of the practice, but there were countless cases where captains in the Royal Navy would duck out of battle with an enemy man-of-war in favor of attacking a defenseless merchant ship. Since there was no way for the admiralty to keep track of locations of ships and no ability for ships to communicate with one another when they were not in sight of each other, the temptation to choose profit before patriotism was a common enough choice and rather easily gotten away with. Wentworth laments that Harville's "luck" in the Mediterranean was not nearly as good as his own, but the reader can only begin to assess the world of meaning that exists between these lines.

During the visit to Lyme, a bond between Wentworth and Louisa Musgrove is blossoming. They play together like children, and Anne is forced to watch. When they approach the high seawall, the flirtatious Louisa insists that Wentworth catch her when she jumps off a stair partway up. To her delight, Wentworth does so. Her giddy emotions then get the best of her as she implores Wentworth to catch her from the very top of the seawall. Wentworth pleads with her to stop because the distance is too great, but his warnings fall on deaf ears. Louisa misses her target and is badly hurt. Beside himself with guilt and anguish, Wentworth notices that Anne keeps her head in the midst of all the confusion and panic. In a telling turn of events, Wentworth looks to Anne for guidance. In that moment he recognizes the depth of substance in Anne Elliot. Anne is capable in a way that the other women are not. She has the attributes of an early feminist character. Wentworth is attracted to her strength of character and ability to keep cool in times of crisis, characteristics that a naval captain would certainly admire in anybody.

While Louisa is on the mend in Lyme, Anne receives a letter from her sister Elizabeth stating that their cousin, William Elliot, has appeared in Bath. The William Elliot link to the story is that though he is a distant family relative, he is the closest male heir to Sir Walter—hence, in accord with the medieval landed-estate law the entail, he is in line to inherit the baronet's property (a situation we've also seen in *Pride and Prejudice* and *Sense and Sensibility*).

Although Anne dreads going, she finally makes her way to Bath to be with her father, sister Elizabeth, and Mrs. Clay, the widowed daughter of Sir Walter's lawyer. Upon arrival, Anne cannot escape the talk about William Elliot, who had embarrassed the family years earlier by marrying a woman who was beneath him (and the Elliots) strictly for her fortune. The woman had since died, and now William has been "pardoned" by Sir Walter. Much of the gossip surrounds his eligibility in marriage for either Elizabeth or Anne. In truth, William is one of Austen's more toxic characters, who is (as we shall see) entirely motivated by greed. He represents the part of the gentry that is the target of Austen's scorn. Everyone but Anne is enamored with him; she alone can see through his charm to his diabolical intentions.

Demonstrating Anne's thoughtfulness and humility, she tracks down an old school friend, Miss Hamilton (now Mrs. Smith), who has been convalescing in Bath. Anne had been very close with the future Mrs. Smith while away at school at age fourteen, a time of loneliness and grief for her late mother. Mrs. Smith's husband, who died two years earlier, had made some money in the colonies, but because he lived in an extravagant manner, he left his affairs in disarray. When Anne finds her, Mrs. Smith is in bad shape. She has practically no income, no servant, is suffering from rheumatic fever, and is temporarily unable to walk. She has come to Bath to take in the therapeutic and healing waters, but because of her situation and her poverty, she has been shunned by Bath society. Therefore, Anne's visit to Mrs. Smith is telling. Anne is a compassionate person, genuine, with no loftiness about her financial status or social ranking. Honorably, she cares for her old friend in need, in spite of the jokes her father and sister make about Anne's former schoolmate who is a nobody to them. Like most of Austen's heroines, Anne has qualities that raise her high above the social-class boundaries that entrap so thoroughly members of her society.

Meanwhile, William Elliot's advances towards the family are on the increase, and it is the opinion of Lady Russell that his intentions are honorable and that his goal is to pursue Anne and not Elizabeth. Lady Russell is correct in her assumptions about William's ambition, but she is dead wrong about his honor. We discover this when gossip about the connection between William and Anne reaches Mrs. Smith through her nurse, Ms. Rooke. Mrs. Smith protects her old friend by informing Anne that she and her husband have had considerable dealings with William Elliot in the past and her assessment of him is that he is a selfish, evil, and completely greedy human being. William was the "trusted" friend of her late husband. At that time, he was rather poor but tried to keep up appearances as a gentleman. Mrs.

Smith's husband Charles was generous with William, and the couple treated him as a member of their family. In addition, William was introduced to Sir Walter Elliot, and the latter tried to take William under his wing. Sir Walter had hoped that William would marry Elizabeth, but William slighted Sir Walter and shied away from the connection. As Mrs. Smith tells it, he was looking for a faster route to fortune, and he found it through marriage to an inferior woman who had riches. William Elliot married for money alone. As proof of her assertions, Mrs. Smith produces a twelve-year-old letter from William to her husband where William is extremely disrespectful.

The gossip then transitions to William's present motives. Mrs. Smith relates that William is worried Sir Walter might form an attachment to the widowed Mrs. Clay, who is spending time with the Elliots in Bath. If Sir Walter and Mrs. Clay were to marry and have a male child, William would be out his inheritance. Mrs. Smith also clarifies that where William did once want nothing to do with the prospect of gaining the title of baronet, he has now changed his opinion and desires to become Sir William Elliot. Furthermore, Anne learns that Mr. Smith was financially ruined by William Elliot's extravagant influence and imprudent encouragement. Mr. Smith had died before he realized that his finances were in ruin. Mrs. Smith had then asked William to be the executor of the will, but he would not assist her. Additionally, Mrs. Smith's husband owned property in the West Indies, but legal issues prevented her from making use of it for profit. She had hoped that William would assist her in sorting out the details, but again he would not help.

After learning all of this poisonous information about William Elliot, the novel takes its final turn and closes in on the climactic moment. A group of characters—including captains Wentworth and Harville, and Mrs. and Admiral Croft—has just arrived in Bath. Emphasizing the way in which Anne and Captain Wentworth have been unable to share their true (and long-repressed) feelings for one another, Anne finds herself in a shop conversing with Captain Harville while Wentworth is nearby composing a letter. The covert letter represents the unspoken love Anne and Wentworth have maintained for each other these eight long years since the captain's first proposal of marriage. Anne doesn't suspect it, but what Wentworth is doing is writing her a second proposal of marriage. He is secretive about his intentions because he lacks confidence in the outcome. Additionally Wentworth is aware of William Elliot's recent advances towards Anne, and fears she might reciprocate his feelings. But Wentworth's love for Anne has increased in her absence, and now he must let it be known.

Captain Wentworth may have been a hero in naval battle, but in his love for Anne Elliot he is timid and awkward. When he finishes the letter, Wentworth and Harville leave the room briefly, but then Wentworth returns claiming shyly that he has forgotten his gloves. Nervously he completes his mission by extending the letter to Anne. When they meet again outside the shop, Anne gives the captain the affirmation he seeks. The couple will indeed be married. In their reunion, they can exult in the love and respect they have for one another—a love that has been building for many years in spite of the social prejudices that temporarily stood in their way.

. . .

As she does so consistently in all of her novels, in *Persuasion* Austen demonstrates the emergence of a portion of the middle class in England when Wentworth, through marriage, is able to increase his social standing. He transitions from the middle class in a "most uncertain profession" to a well-monied naval captain, and now he will increase his social standing all the more by marrying the daughter of a baronet. Writes Austen: "Captain Wentworth, with five-and-twenty thousand pounds, and as high in his profession as merit and activity could place him, was no longer nobody. He was now esteemed quite worthy to address the daughter of a foolish, spendthrift baronet." Austen's Romantic hero has achieved a marriage that is both ethically sound, monetarily healthy, and of a rank which places him in the lower echelon of the gentry.

In addition Wentworth is able to act for Mrs. Smith in settling her legal entanglements involving her property in the West Indies. This is an important detail as it positions Wentworth as someone who now has authority both at home in England and abroad in the colonial arena. He is a new breed of Englishman. A century earlier he would have been looked down upon in society. But now that money is competing with social rank, Wentworth finds that his agency is waxing, while that of members of the lower level gentry (someone like William Elliot, for example) is waning. Austen demonstrates the emergence of this new and valuable category of man in society when she describes Wentworth's efforts in helping Mrs. Smith: "[Mrs. Smith] was their earliest visitor in their settled life;

147

and Captain Wentworth, by putting her in the way of recovering her husband's property in the West Indies, by writing for her, acting for her, and seeing her through all the petty difficulties of the case, with the activity and exertion of a fearless man and a determined friend, fully requited the services which she had rendered, or ever meant to render, to his wife." Such active language and sense of authority demonstrate a changing of the guard. Wentworth is able to accomplish for Mrs. Smith what the "gentleman" William Elliot can't do. Wentworth is heroic and part of a new England where connections, actions, and monetary success in the colonial realm are now of valued importance.

The union between Wentworth and Anne also provides an example of a new kind of marriage that is based on love and partnership rather than status and finances. The couple will be extremely comfortable with Anne's dowry and Wentworth's prize money in the bank; however, in Austen's world, material gain is icing on the cake. The true reward for the couple will be their companionable marriage. The 1995 Sony Pictures film version of *Persuasion* starring Amanda Root and Ciarán Hinds concludes with Anne accompanying her husband on a voyage at sea. Presumably Wentworth is involved in some kind of colonial administration. Although Austen doesn't end her novel in the same manner, the moment echoes Sophia Croft's conversation about accompanying her husband on many of his voyages at sea. This favorable depiction applauds husband and wife for their adventurous natures and their intense desire to be together. More so, however, we can applaud the husband for his open-minded willingness to have his wife accompany him in a world that is still repressively patriarchal. And we can applaud even louder the wife for her pioneering desire to expand boundaries for early nineteenth-century women. Indeed, this couple will live happily ever after.

# Chapter 8

*Jane Austen's Legacy*

Jane Austen is arguably the most widely popular literary author studied today in the academic classroom. Feminists have identified with the strength of her female characters, literary historians have explored Austen's England and its relationship to empire, and other critics have paid close attention to the provocative social-class issues that are woven into each of her plots. Yet beyond these academic perspectives for accessing Austen, her novels are simply entertaining, and modern audiences identify with her characters and situations. For these reasons, Austen has been embraced beyond the hallowed halls of academe. In their collection of essays entitled *Jane Austen and Co.: Remaking the Past in Contemporary Culture,*

Suzanne R. Pucci and James Thompson refer to the proliferation of Austen-related films, remakes, spinoffs, web resources, tourism, and Janeite products as "Austenmania," a "virtual industry" of Austen production and money-making in the United States, Great Britain, and around the world. Since Austen's novels are so preoccupied with money and the rise of the middle class, Austen herself would likely enjoy the knowledge that her work has generated such a frenzy of material production. There is no other literary novelist who is appreciated by such a wide spectrum of fans.

Jane Austen's legacy is an immense and ever-expanding universe. That said, it is important here at the close of *Jane Austen for Beginners* to assess some of the ways that Austen's life and works continue to reverberate and echo in modern culture. When she lived and wrote, Austen's world was largely bounded by a small stretch of territory in the south of England. Her reach was also limited due to constraints placed on women of her time. Miraculously, however, the stories she crafted two hundred years ago have engaged and will continue to engage huge audiences around the globe.

The most powerful aspect of the Austen legacy is Jane's defiant and persistent desire to be a writer. During Austen's lifetime, England was in the dark ages in terms of providing challenging academic opportunities for women. Privileged males who went to school and eventually to college received a highly rigorous classical education, where they learned all major disciples. If a woman attended a school at all, it was more of a finishing school, where she would have been able to refine her talents and manners, thereby increasing her ability to attract a husband. Next to bearing children, this was a woman's primary goal in life. If she was unmarried or had no money, a woman might consider the professions of governess or school teacher, but most women certainly did not dream of becoming published authors! In this regard especially, Austen is a role model. She is so important to us because she is a pioneer—especially for women. Against the social pressures of her day to marry and have children, Austen fought for her profession as author.

In addition to her persistent desire to write, Jane Austen is a rebel for the way in which she depicted the institution of marriage. Matrimony is central to all the Austen novels. Marriages more often than not during Austen's time were like arranged marriages. Families would marry off their sons and daughters as a kind of alliance to keep land and money intact between families. Young men and women living in isolated areas did not have many options for partners. Thus family alliances (you've heard of "kissing cousins") were more common than not. Austen defies this marriage tradition. She defied conventions in her own life by refusing a proposal made to her, and she defied it in her novels. Several of her characters refuse proposals of marriage, and all of her female protagonists refuse to settle for loveless marriages. This may not seem outrageous to modern readers, but the act of refusal was radical and unpopular in Jane Austen's day.

As well, Austen is important to us because in spite of her limited field of vision, she was able to access a world beyond the domestic spaces of her novels. Nineteenth-century women inhabited what is called the private realm in society—that is, the home and hearth. Women were expected to be domestic, delicate, and dedicated to all things related to the family. Men, on the other hand, existed in the public realm, charged with being the doers in society. Men took care of the business, belonged to clubs, drank and gambled, hunted, went to war, traveled, and oversaw farming on their properties and affairs on their estates. Written from the female perspective, Austen's novels all take place in locations that are part of the private realm. We learn about the off-stage doings of the male characters while we are on stage in the domestic places of women. In *Mansfield Park*, for example, the reader cannot follow Thomas Bertram to Antigua when he looks after his sugar plantation. The reader stays at home and learns about his doings via communications through letters and gossip. Yet, in spite of these limited points of view, the reach of Austen's novels extends far outside the family sitting room. Conversation in the private realm reminds us that just outside that sphere the Industrial Revolution is getting underway, war is being fought, and the British Empire is expanding. Windows in Austen's texts provide us access. We are not on location in Antigua with Thomas Bertram, but we see how the ripple effects of empire-building are experienced back home in England and in the private realms of the women who inhabit the domestic spaces.

Austen also reveals a society that has much in common with our own consumer culture, where economic fates can change suddenly and dramatically for the better and for the worse. This is yet another reason why her novels have become so extremely popular with modern American and British audiences. In our own American culture, we are not fixed or stuck in our positions on the social ladder. Like us, Austen's characters, and members of her own family, could climb up the social ladder through marriage, business, trade, or military success. Think of the character Bingley from *Pride and Prejudice*, who is not of landed-gentry stock like his best friend Darcy, but who has made a great fortune for himself via trade and can afford to live the life of a gentleman. Think of Austen's brother Francis, who rose as high in the ranks of the navy as was possible and died wealthy at the age of 91. Or think of Austen's brother Henry, who early on achieved an elite social status as a successful banker only to lose it all to bankruptcy later in his career. Two centuries after Austen's novels were published, we continue to identify—perhaps now more than ever—with the social-class issues she presents.

But Austen's greatest legacy is the love story. Each of her novels presents us with romantic scenarios between characters that we care deeply about. Time and time again, we are introduced to plots that weave together tension, uncertainty, and frustration only to culminate in total satisfaction. We love the love story, and Austen is a master at telling it. In our contemporary world where romantic behavior between couples can be anything but subtle, many find appealing the portrait in Austen's work of a time when manners and decorum were polite. Austen hailed from an age when a look, a gentle touch, or a word in passing could hold a universe of meaning. These subtleties engage and excite our imaginations. Her romances distract us from our busy lives and enable us—if only briefly—to understand and appreciate the meaning of true, unconditional love.

. . .

In a general sense, Jane Austen's novels are so popular with a wide spectrum of modern readers and scholars because her stories present us with many levels of interpretation. You may read her work without paying such close attention to the historical aspects, and your experience will be thoroughly enjoyable; however, you can always dig deeper. Every level of interpretation is valid and gratifying. And if you are willing, Austen will help you go further into her world. Her legacy is the writing that she left us. Her work continues to resonate with modern-day readers because of its depth and relevance. And for teachers, students, and general readers, Austen's novels facilitate learning about both Austen's England and the wider world that surrounds it. We read them for the richness of knowledge that they provide, and we enjoy them because they are smart, funny, challenging, and useful.

Beyond the six novels that Jane Austen left us, how do we explain the many hundreds of Austen-related books, films, spinoffs, and web resources that continue to appear daily on bookshelves, on the Internet, in movie theaters, and on TV screens? Austen wrote an estimated 1500 pages of fictional text, and yet, judging by the unending production of new Austen-related fiction (consider the popularity of Seth Grahame-Smith's 2009 parody novel *Pride and Prejudice and Zombies*, or esteemed English mystery writer P.D. James' bestselling 2011 novel *Death Comes to Pemberley*), it seems we want to keep her career up and running for 150,000 more pages. Why are the six novels not enough? Why do we keep writing more Jane? There is no clearcut answer. Perhaps we can't get enough of the love story; perhaps we long for times that were simpler. Since Austen died prematurely at age 41, in the prime of her writing career, perhaps we want to correct the tragedy that nature committed in taking her life too soon; or perhaps we seek to rediscover our favorite author in our speculations about what she would have written next or what was contained in those thousands of letters that Cassandra destroyed. Whatever the reason, the fact remains that the Jane Austen formula has become an industry; she makes money, she excites imaginations, and we can't leave her alone.

The list of Austen-inspired texts, films, and resources that follows is evidence that though Jane Austen may be gone from this world, she is not forgotten. Look on fellow Janeite, and feast your eyes on a lifetime of reading and viewing pleasure. I hope you will be impressed that this multi-page list is all the result of a modest vision created by a provincial woman from a small village in the south of England, who never wandered far from her birthplace.

# Jane Austen in Popular Culture

## A (Partial) List

## Film and Television Adaptations of Jane Austen's Novels:

### Sense and Sensibility

Television Miniseries (1971)

Television Miniseries (1981)

Feature Film (Emma Thompson, Kate Winslet; 1995)

Television Miniseries (2008)

*Kandukondain Kandukondain*— "Bollywood" Feature Film, based on the novel (2000)

### Pride and Prejudice

Television Film (1938)

Feature Film (Laurence Olivier, Greer Garson; 1940)

Television Miniseries (1952)

*Orgoglio e Pregudizio* Television Miniseries (1957)

Television Miniseries (1958)

*De vier dochters Bennet* Television Miniseries (1961)

Television Miniseries (1967)

Television Miniseries (1980)

Television Miniseries (1995)

Feature Film (Keira Knightley, Donald Sutherland; 2005)

*You've Got Mail*—Feature Film, inspired by the novel (1998)

*Bridget Jones's Diary*—Feature Film, inspired by the novel (2001)

*Pride and Prejudice: A Latter-Day Comedy*— Feature Film, updating the novel (2003)

*Bride and Prejudice*— "Bollywood" Feature Film, based on the novel (2004)

*Lost in Austen*—Television Miniseries, inspired by the novel (2008)

## Mansfield Park

Television Miniseries (1983)

Feature Film (Frances O'Connor, Jonny Lee Miller; 1999)

Television Miniseries (2007)

## Emma

Feature Film (1948)

6-Part Television Series (1960)

6-Part Television Series (1972)

Feature Film (Gwyneth Paltrow, Ewan McGregor; 1996)

Television Film (Kate Beckinsale, 1996)

4-Part Television Series (2009)

*Clueless*—Feature Film, inspired by the novel (1995)

## Northanger Abbey

Television Film (1986)

Television Film (2007)

### Persuasion

Television Miniseries (1960)

Television Miniseries (1971)

Television Film (Amanda Root, Ciarán Hinds; 1995)

Television Film (2007)

## Austen-Related Feature Films:

*The Jane Austen Book Club* (2007)

*Becoming Jane* (Anne Hathaway, James McAvoy; 2007)

*Jane Austen in Manhattan* (Anne Baxter, 1980)

## Austen-Related Books

### Paranormal

*Emma and the Werewolves* by Jane Austen and Adam Rann

*Jane Bites Back: A Novel* by Michael Thomas Ford

*Mansfield Park and Mummies* by Jane Austen and Vera Nazarian

*Mr. Darcy, Vampyre* by Amanda Grange

*The Phantom of Pemberley: A Pride & Prejudice Murder Mystery* by Regina Jeffers

*Pride, Prejudice & Zombies* by Seth Grahame-Smith

*Sense, Sensibility & Sea Monsters* by Jane Austen and Ben H. Winters

### Sense & Sensibility Spinoffs

*Colonel Brandon's Diary* by Amanda Grange

*Miss Lucy Steele* by Ruth Berger

*The Third Sister: A Novel That Continues What Jane Austen's Sense and Sensibility Began* by Julia Barrett

*Willoughby's Return: A Tale of Almost Irresistible Temptation* by Jane Odiwe

### *Pride & Prejudice* Spinoffs

*Apprehension and Desire* by Ola Wegner and Janusz Wilcznski

*Darcy & Elizabeth: Nights and Days at Pemberley* by Linda Berdoll

*The Darcy Cousins* by Monica Fairview

*The Darcys & the Bingleys: A Tale of Two Gentlemen's Marriages to Two Most Devoted Sisters* by Marsha Altman

*Darcy's Temptation: A Sequel to Jane Austen's Pride & Prejudice* by Regina Jeffers

*Death Comes to Pemberley,* by P.D. James

*The Exploits & Adventures of Miss Alethea Darcy* by Elizabeth Aston

*Fate and Consequences* by Linda Wells

*First Impressions: A Tale of Less Pride & Prejudice* by Alexa Adams

*Impulse & Initiative: What If Mr. Darcy Had Set Out To Win Elizabeth's Heart* by Abigail Reynolds

*Longbourn's Unexpected Matchmaker* by Emma Hox

*Loving Mr. Darcy: Journeys Beyond Pemberley* by Sharon Lathan

*Memory Volume 1: Lasting Impressions* by Linda Wells

*Memory Volume 2: Trials to Bear* by Linda Wells

*Memory Volume 3: How Far We Have Come* by Linda Wells

*Mr. Darcy Presents His Bride: A Sequel to Jane Austen's Pride & Prejudice* by Helen Halstead

*Mr. Darcy's Daughters* by Elizabeth Aston

*Mr. Darcy's Decision: A Sequel to Jane Austen's Pride & Prejudice* by Juliette Shapiro

*Mr. Darcy's Great Escape: A Tale of the Darcys & the Bingleys* by Marsha Altman

*Mr. Darcy Takes a Wife* by Linda Berdoll

*My Dearest Mr. Darcy* by Sharon Lathan

*A Noteworthy Courtship* by Laura Sanchez

*The Other Mr. Darcy* by Monica Fairview

*Pemberley Shades: Pride and Prejudice Continues* by D. A. Bonavia-Hunt

*The Plight of the Darcy Brothers* by Marsha Altman

*Rainy Days* by Lory Lilian

*The Second Mrs. Darcy* by Elizabeth Aston

*To Conquer Mr. Darcy* by Abigail Reynolds

*The True Darcy Spirit* by Elizabeth Aston

### *Mansfield Park* Spinoffs

*Edmund Bertram's Diary* by Amanda Grange

*Eliza's Daughter* by Joan Aiken

*The Matters at Mansfield: Or, The Crawford Affair* by Carrie Bebris

*Mansfield Park Revisited* by Joan Aiken

*Murder at Mansfield Park* by Lynn Shepherd

*The Watsons and Emma Watson: Jane Austen's Unfinished Novel*, completed by Joan Aiken

*The Youngest Miss Ward* by Joan Aiken


### Emma Spinoffs

*Chance Encounters* by Linda Wells

*Deception: A Tale of Pride and Prejudice* by Ola Wegner and Janusz Wilcznski

*Emma and Knightley: Perfect Happiness in Highbury* by Rachel Billington

*George Knightley, Esquire: Charity Envieth Not* by Barbara Cornthwaite

*Intrigue at Highbury: Or, Emma's Match* by Carrie Bebris

*James Fairfax* by Jane Austen and Adam Campan

*Jane Fairfax: The Secret Story of the Second Heroine in Jane Austen's Emma* by Joan Aiken

*Mr. Knightley's Diary* by Amanda Grange

*Mrs. Elton in America: The Compleat Mrs. Elton* by Diana Birchall

*Remembrance of the Past* by Lory Lilian

*A Visit to Highbury* by Joan Austen-Leigh


### Persuasion Spinoffs

*Captain Wentworth's Diary* by Amanda Grange

*Captain Wentworth's Persuasion: Jane Austen's Classic Retold Through His Eyes* by Regina Jeffers


162

*For You Alone ( Frederick Wentworth, Captain, Book 2)* by Susan Kaye

*Mercy's Embrace: Elizabeth Elliot's Story, Book 1 — So Rough a Course* by Laura Hile

*Mercy's Embrace: Elizabeth Elliot's Story, Book 2 — So Lively a Chase* by Laura Hile

*Mercy's Embrace: Elizabeth Elliot's Story, Book 3 — The Lady Must Decide* by Laura Hile

*None but You (Frederick Wentworth, Captain, Book 1)* by Susan Kaye

## Lady Susan Spinoff

*Lady Vernon and Her Daughter: A Novel of Jane Austen's Lady Susan* by Jane Rubino and Caitlen Rubino-Bradway

## Austen-Inspired Fiction (Contemporary Settings)

*According to Jane* by Marilyn Brant

*A Little Bit Psychic: Pride and Prejudice with a Modern Twist* by Aimee Avery

*Amanda (The Austen Series, Book 5)* by Debra White Smith

*Central Park (The Austen Series, Book 3)* by Debra White Smith

*First Impressions (The Austen Series, Book 1)* by Debra White Smith

*The Importance of Being Emma* by Juliet Archer

*Jane Austen Ruined My Life* by Beth Pattillo

*Love, Lies and Lizzie* by Rosie Rushton

*The Man Who Loved Pride & Prejudice: A Modern Love Story With A Jane Austen Twist* by Abigail Reynolds

*Me and Mr. Darcy* by Alexandra Potter

*Mr. Darcy Broke My Heart* by Beth Pattillo

*Northanger Alibi* by Jenni James

*Northpointe Chalet (The Austen Series, Book 4)* by Debra White Smith

*Perfect Fit: A Modern Tale of Pride and Prejudice* by Linda Wells

*Persuading Annie* by Melissa Nathan

*Possibilities (The Austen Series, Book 6)* by Debra White Smith

*Pride, Prejudice and Jasmin Field* by Melissa Nathan

*Reason and Romance (The Austen Series, Book 2)* by Debra White Smith

*Secret Schemes and Daring Dreams* by Rosie Rushton

*Seducing Mr. Darcy* by Gwyn Cready

*Vanity and Vexation* by Kate Fenton

## *Jane Austen Websites and Blogs*

austen.com
austenblog.com
austenfans.com
findingjaneausten.com
janeausten.ac.uk (Jane Austen Fiction Manuscripts)
janeaustenaddict.com
janeaustenba.org (Jane Austen Society of Buenos Aires)
janeaustenbooks.net
janeaustenfan.blogspot.com
janeaustenfans.livejournal.com
janeausteninvermont.com (Jane Austen Society of North America, Vermont region)
janeausten.org
janeausten.co.uk (Jane Austen Centre, Bath, England)
jane-austens-house-museum.org.uk (Jane Austen's House Museum)
janeaustensoci.freeuk.com (The Jane Austen Society of the United Kingdom)

janeaustensworld.wordpress.com
janitesonthejames.com (Jane Austen Today)
jasa.net.au (Jane Austen Society of Australia)
jasna.org (Jane Austen Society of North America)
themaindenscourt.blogspot.com/2010/05/jane-austen-spin-offs-
    and-sequels.html
pemberley.com (The Republic of Pemberley)
seekingjaneausten.com
talklikejaneausten.com
veryjaneausten.com

## *Bibliography and Further Reading*

Ashton, T. S. *An Economic History of England: The Eighteenth Century*. Lexington: University Press of Kentucky, 1986. Print.

Austen, Jane. *Catherine and Other Writings*. Oxford: Oxford UP, 1993. Print.

—. *Emma*. 1815. London and New York: W. W. Norton, 2000. Norton Critical Edition. Print.

—. *Jane Austen's Letters*. Philadelphia: Pavilion, 2003. Print.

—. *Juvenilia*. Cambridge: 1787-1793. Cambridge Scholars Publishing, 2008. Print.

—. *Lady Susan*. 1794. Mineola, NY: Dover, 2005. Print.

—. *Mansfield Park*. 1814. London and New York: W. W. Norton, 1998. Norton Critical Edition. Print.

—. *Northanger Abbey*. 1818. London and New York, 2004. Norton Critical Edition. Print.

—. *Persuasion*. 1818. London and New York: W. W. Norton, 1995. Norton Critical Edition. Print.

—. *Pride and Prejudice*. 1813. New York: W. W. Norton, 2001. Norton Critical Edition. Print.

—. *Sanditon*. 1817. New York: Simon and Schuster, 1975. Print.

—. *Sense and Sensibility.* 1811. New York: W. W. Norton, 2002. Norton Critical Edition. Print.

Austen, Henry Thomas. "Biographical Notice." *Northanger Abbey and Persuasion.* London: John Murray, 1818. Print.

Austen-Leigh, James Edward and R. W. Chapman. *A Memoir of Jane Austen And Other Family Recollections.* Oxford: The Clarendon Press, 1926. Print.

Barry, Jonathan, and Christopher Brooks, eds. *The Middling Sort of People: Culture, Society and Politics in England, 1550–1800.* New York: St. Martin's Press, 1994. Print.

Baynham, Henry. *From the Lower Deck: The Royal Navy, 1780–1840.* Barre, MA: Barre Publishers, 1970. Print.

Bellamy, Liz. *Commerce, Morality and the Eighteenth-Century Novel.* Cambridge: Cambridge University Press, 1998. Print.

Black, Jeremy and Philip Woodfine, eds. *The British Navy and Use of Naval Power in the Eighteenth Century.* Atlantic Highlands: Humanities Press, 1989. Print.

Brown, Julia Prewitt. *Jane Austen's Novels: Social Change and Literary Form.* Cambridge and London: Harvard University Press, 1979. Print.

Copeland, Edward, and Juliet McMaster, eds. *The Cambridge Companion to Jane Austen.* Cambridge: Cambridge University Press, 1997. Print.

—. *Women Writing About Money: Women's Fiction in England, 1790–1820.* Cambridge: Cambridge University Press, 1995. Print.

Copley, Stephen. *Literature and the Social Order in Eighteenth-Century England.* London and Dover: Croom Helm, 1984. Print.

Dryden, Robert G. "Did Jane Know Jack Tar: Assessing the Significance of Austen's Other Navy." *1650-1850: Ideas, Aesthetics, and Inquiries in the Early Modern Era.* 17 (2010): 205-25. Print.

—. " 'Luck be a Lady Tonight': Jane Austen's Precarious Idealization of Naval Heroes in *Persuasion.*" *1650-1850: Ideas, Aesthetics, and Inquiries in the Early Modern Era* 13 (2006): 91-115. Print.

—. "Reading and Teaching Our Way Out of Jane Austen Novels (Naval Options)." *Persuasions: The Jane Austen Journal* 27 (2005): 208-18. Print.

Earle, Peter. *The Making of the English Middle Class: Business, Society and Family Life in London, 1660–1730.* Berkeley: University of California Press, 1989. Print.

Greenfield, Susan. *Mothering Daughters: Novels and the Politics of Family Romance, From Frances Burney to Jane Austen.* Detroit: Wayne State UP, 2002. Print.

Harman, Claire. *Jane's Fame: How Jane Austen Conquered the World.* New York: Henry Holt, 2009. Print.

Honan, Park. *Jane Austen: Her Life.* London: Weidenfield and Nicolson, 1987. Print.

Hubback, J. H. & E. C. *Jane Austen's Sailor Brothers: Being the Adventures of Sir Francis Austen, G.C.B., Admiral of the Fleet and Rear-Admiral Charles Austen.* Stroud: Ian Hodgkins; Westport: Meckler, 1986. Print.

"Jane Austen in Popular Culture." *Wikipedia.* 24 July, 2011. Web. 1 July, 2011.

Johnson, Claudia L. *Jane Austen: Women, Politics, and the Novel.* Chicago: UP Chicago, 1988. Print.

Lane, Maggie. "Daily Life in Jane Austen's England." *Emma.* Ed. Stephen M. Parrish. New York: W. W. Norton, 2000. 342-47. Print.

Langford, Paul. *The Eighteenth-Century, 1688–1815.* New York: St. Martin's Press, 1976. Print.

—. *A Polite and Commercial People: England, 1727–1783.* Oxford: Clarendon Press, 1989. Print.

Lewis, Michael. *A Social History of the Navy, 1793–1815*. London: George Allen & Unwin, 1960. Print.

*Lost in Austen*. Dir. Dan Zeff. Perf. Jemima Rooper, Elliot Cowan. Mammoth Screen, Ltd, 2008. Film.

Macdonald, Gina, and Andrew F. Macdonald, eds. *Jane Austen on Screen*. Cambridge: Cambridge UP, 2003. Print.

Neale, R. S. *Bath 1680–1850: A Social History, or A Valley of Pleasure, Yet a Sink of Iniquity*. Boston and London: Routledge & Kegan Paul, 1981. Print.

—. *Class in English History, 1680–1850*. Totowa: Barnes and Noble, 1981. Print.

Parrill, Sue. *Jane Austen on Film and Television: A Critical Study of the Adaptations*. Jefferson, NC and London: McFarland, 2002. Print.

Parrish, Stephen M. "Preface to Third Edition." *Emma*. New York: W. W. Norton, 2000. vii-ix. Print.

Porter, Roy. *English Society in the Eighteenth Century*. 1982. London and New York: Penguin, 1990. Print.

Pucci, Suzanne R, and James Thompson, eds. *Jane Austen and Co., Remaking the Past in Contemporary Culture*. Albany: SUNY UP, 2003. Print.

R. Heather. "The Maiden's Court: Jane Austen Spin Offs and Sequels." Web. 1 July, 2011.

Reeve, Katharine. *Jane Austen in Bath: Walking Tours of the Writer's City*. New York: The Little Bookroom, 2006. Print.

Roberts, Warren. *Jane Austen and the French Revolution*. New York: St. Martins, 1979. Print.

Rodger, N. A. M. *The Wooden World: An Anatomy of the Georgian Navy*. New York: W. W. Norton, 1986. Print.

Rule, John. *Albion's People: English Society, 1714–1815*. London and New York: Longman, 1992. Print.

Said, Edward W. *Culture and Imperialism*. New York: Vintage, 1994. Print.

Southam, Brian. *Jane Austen and the Navy*. London: Hambledon and London, 2000. Print.

Speck, W. A. *Literature and Society in Eighteenth-Century England: Ideology, Politics and Culture, 1680–1820*. London and New York: Longman, 1998. Print.

Spence, Jon. *Becoming Jane Austen*. London: Continuum, 2003. Print.

Spring, David. *European Landed Elites in the Nineteenth Century*. Baltimore: Johns Hopkins UP, 1977. Print.

Stone, Lawrence. *The Family, Sex and Marriage in England, 1500-1800*. New York: Harper and Row, 1977. Print.

Tomalin, Claire. *Jane Austen: A Life*. New York: Vintage, 1997. Print.

Troost, Linda, and Sayre Greenfield, eds. *Jane Austen in Hollywood*. Lexington: UP Kentucky, 2001. Print.

Tuite, Clara. *Romantic Austen: Sexual Politics and the Literary Canon*. Cambridge: Cambridge UP, 2002. Print.

Williamson, Samuel H. *Measuring Worth*. 2011. Web. July 1, 2011. Print.

Wiltshire, John. *Recreating Jane Austen*. Cambridge: Cambridge UP, 2001. Print.

Woolf, Virginia. *A Room of One's Own*. 1929. New York: Harcourt, 1989.

# THE FOR BEGINNERS® SERIES

| | |
|---|---|
| AFRICAN HISTORY FOR BEGINNERS: | ISBN 978-1-934389-18-8 |
| ANARCHISM FOR BEGINNERS: | ISBN 978-1-934389-32-4 |
| ARABS & ISRAEL FOR BEGINNERS: | ISBN 978-1-934389-16-4 |
| ART THEORY FOR BEGINNERS: | ISBN 978-934389-47-8 |
| ASTRONOMY FOR BEGINNERS: | ISBN 978-934389-25-6 |
| AYN RAND FOR BEGINNERS: | ISBN 978-1-934389-37-9 |
| BARACK OBAMA FOR BEGINNERS, AN ESSENTIAL GUIDE: | ISBN 978-1-934389-44-7 |
| BLACK HISTORY FOR BEGINNERS: | ISBN 978-1-934389-19-5 |
| THE BLACK HOLOCAUST FOR BEGINNERS: | ISBN 978-1-934389-03-4 |
| BLACK WOMEN FOR BEGINNERS: | ISBN 978-1-934389-20-1 |
| CHOMSKY FOR BEGINNERS: | ISBN 978-1-934389-17-1 |
| DADA & SURREALISM FOR BEGINNERS: | ISBN 978-1-934389-00-3 |
| DANTE FOR BEGINNERS: | ISBN 978-1-934389-67-6 |
| DECONSTRUCTION FOR BEGINNERS: | ISBN 978-1-934389-26-3 |
| DEMOCRACY FOR BEGINNERS: | ISBN 978-1-934389-36-2 |
| DERRIDA FOR BEGINNERS: | ISBN 978-1-934389-11-9 |
| EASTERN PHILOSOPHY FOR BEGINNERS: | ISBN 978-1-934389-07-2 |
| EXISTENTIALISM FOR BEGINNERS: | ISBN 978-1-934389-21-8 |
| FDR AND THE NEW DEAL FOR BEGINNERS: | ISBN 978-1-934389-50-8 |
| FOUCAULT FOR BEGINNERS: | ISBN 978-1-934389-12-6 |
| GLOBAL WARMING FOR BEGINNERS: | ISBN 978-1-934389-27-0 |
| HEIDEGGER FOR BEGINNERS: | ISBN 978-1-934389-13-3 |
| ISLAM FOR BEGINNERS: | ISBN 978-1-934389-01-0 |
| JUNG FOR BEGINNERS: | ISBN 978-1-934389-76-8 |
| KIERKEGAARD FOR BEGINNERS: | ISBN 978-1-934389-14-0 |
| LACAN FOR BEGINNERS: | ISBN 978-1-934389-39-3 |
| LINGUISTICS FOR BEGINNERS: | ISBN 978-1-934389-28-7 |
| MALCOLM X FOR BEGINNERS: | ISBN 978-1-934389-04-1 |
| MARX'S *DAS KAPITAL* FOR BEGINNERS: | ISBN 978-1-934389-59-1 |
| NIETZSCHE FOR BEGINNERS: | ISBN 978-1-934389-05-8 |
| THE OLYMPICS FOR BEGINNERS: | ISBN 978-1-934389-33-1 |
| PHILOSOPHY FOR BEGINNERS: | ISBN 978-1-934389-02-7 |
| PLATO FOR BEGINNERS: | ISBN 978-1-934389-08-9 |
| POETRY FOR BEGINNERS: | ISBN 978-1-934389-46-1 |
| POSTMODERNISM FOR BEGINNERS: | ISBN 978-1-934389-09-6 |
| RELATIVITY & QUANTUM PHYSICS FOR BEGINNERS | ISBN 978-1-934389-42-3 |
| SARTRE FOR BEGINNERS: | ISBN 978-1-934389-15-7 |
| SHAKESPEARE FOR BEGINNERS: | ISBN 978-1-934389-29-4 |
| STRUCTURALISM & POSTSTRUCTURALISM FOR BEGINNERS: | ISBN 978-1-934389-10-2 |
| WOMEN'S HISTORY FOR BEGINNERS: | ISBN 978-1-934389-60-7 |
| U.S. CONSTITUTION FOR BEGINNERS: | ISBN 978-1-934389-62-1 |
| ZEN FOR BEGINNERS: | ISBN 978-1-934389-06-5 |
| ZINN FOR BEGINNERS: | ISBN 978-1-934389-40-9 |

www.forbeginnersbooks.com